CARLOS GARDEL

The voice of the tango

RAFAEL FLORES MONTENEGRO

CARLOS GARDEL

The voice of the tango

Image Archive: Mundo Gardeliano
Discography production and control: Manuel Llano Pérez
Translator: Donald Snowden
Style correction: Silvia García Rey y
Santiago García Rey
Graphic design: Pablo Garriga

First Spanish edition: Alianza Editorial, S. A., Madrid,
España, 2003.

Second Spanish edition Ediciones Fabro, Buenos Aires,
Argentina, 2016.

First English edition. Corrected and increased;
Mundo Gardeliano Editions, Los Angeles, USA, 2019

TABLE OF CONTENTS

SECOND PART

THIRD PART

ABOUT THE AUTHOR, RAFAEL FLORES MONTENEGRO

An Argentinean writer living in Spain since 1979, Rafael Flores Montenegro could be one of the characters drawn from his own literary creations, a body of work encompassing **poetry, short stories, novels and essays** written with a great creative sensibility. A tireless student of the world and human condition through language and images, his writings range from the rational to the absurd, from fantasy to dreamlike. These are texts we can make our own in a flash or simply admire from a distance, but they never fail to move us.

He has shared him insights in the various literary workshops he has given in Madrid since 1990, as well as any number of conferences held at universities and cultural institutions on both sides of the Atlantic.

His literary work doesn't shy away from his life experience as an active militant in Argentina and subsequent exile in Spain during the 1970s and 1980s. His writing during this period bears an impassioned witness that is impossible to dismiss. His arguments display an unwavering conviction in tenacious defense of a better life for the most disadvantaged classes, in favor of human rights and against social injustice. A commitment that is revealed to the reader subtly and with a masterful literary flair that

distances it from a mere direct accusation, making it more effective for his purposes.

At the same he has enthusiastically devoted himself to **spreading the word about tango**, which he explores with an emotional gravity to match his literary flair.

We begin with the tango "Nel Mezzo del Cammin di Nostra Vita', back in the 1980s. Publications, books, radio, shows, recordings, dance sessions of all kinds -from those held in alternative spaces right up to the ones that took place at the Ritz Hotel-, television documentaries, conferences... Since that time, we felt that 'the tango was making its comeback heard".

He has published several books on tango in Spanish, but also translated into Italian, German, French, Vietnamese, and now English. He contributes regularly to the specialist press and magazines, both Spanish and Latin American.

Since the late '80s, he has shared his knowledge and research about tango culture over the Spanish radio airwaves, collaborating with various broadcasters for over 30 years: Radio Cadena Española, RNE Radio 4, Onda Madrid, Radio Voz and RNE Radio

5 until September 2018. He is equally involved in giving lectures at conferences and organizing seminars and workshops. In addition to his work as musical director for singers and dancers, he collaborates on the release of recordings and compilations of classic older pieces.

He possesses one of the most complete musical, film, and literary collections about tango and folklore that we can find. He has been collecting his materials from a wide variety of sources encountered throughout his extensive career of research, the fruits of his embrace of a life lived investigating and learning.

Taking the existence of the tango into account is unavoidable for understanding the 20th century. The movies indicate that and giving exposure to the style of dancing arm-in-arm -a fundamental discovery of the tango world- in turn was incorporated into other contemporary genres. It is unavoidable when speaking of Madrid, Barcelona, Milan, New York.... not just Buenos Aires and Montevideo.

The tango is no stranger to the central phenomena of modern times: migrations, cultural blends, globalization, styles and fashions, and inventions to be grateful for like records and photography. It knows about our impulse to live beyond all restrictions, our finite lifespan, the desires to raise ourselves up from the mud from which we are made.

Perhaps, without overstating the case, it embodies the genuine contemporary written poetry of the street.

He received the 1997 SADAIC prize for promotion of Argentinean music and literature in Europe.

INTRODUCTION

CARLOS GARDEL (1890-1935) occupies a unique place in the popular culture of Latin America. From humble beginnings, he rose to become one of the first superstars of the Latin world. His sudden, unexpected death in an airplane crash in 1935 was front page news in the press around the planet.

The tango was at the peak of its popularity during those years and Gardel recorded one classic tango after another that reinforced his status as a musical idol in Argentina and Uruguay. From 1923 on, he performed on successful tours in Madrid, Barcelona, and Paris, where he filmed the movies that quickly earned him widespread international acclaim and fame. One interesting anecdote we discovered was that the Spanish-speaking audience on both sides of the Atlantic forced the projectionist to rewind the film to repeat the scenes that featured Gardel singing. He went on to produce his own Spanish-language films in New York, and at the time of his death, Hollywood was already planning to launch him to stardom in the English language screen.

Of the hundreds of books written about him, very few can properly be called biographies. Gardel had such a rich and eventful life, that very few authors dared to write a book covering the tango artist's whole life. One man who takes on the challenge is Rafael Flores Montenegro, a native of Argentina who has lived most of his life in Spain. After many years devoted to Spanish language poetry and literature, he threw himself into the world of tango in books, conferences, seminars, and radio programs. "Carlos Gardel, the Voice of the Tango" was his third work to include an essay on the singer's life and career. It is the result of many years of research. With interest in Gardel clearly on the rise since the worldwide success of Gardel's tango anthem *Por una Cabeza*, the Spanish-language edition was published several times in Spain and Argentina.

The book you hold in your hand is the first English translation to appear following the noteworthy biography by Simon Collier in 1985. This book adds well-documented facts about Gardel's life, including new information unearthed by various investigators since 1985. It is illustrated with images provided by "Mundo Gardeliano" of Los Angeles, probably the single most complete database about the singer in the world.

We are confident this book will be of great value for all those readers outside the Spanish-speaking world who are interested in Carlos Gardel.

César Fratantoni

FIRST PART

1. THE ORIGINS OF TANGO

When we say tango, we understand the word to encompass over a century of culture that includes music, dance, song... rioplatense culture with a worldwide appeal that continues to spread to the present day.

The word tango sounds clearly African to us. Its history appears linked to enclosed quarters where black slaves were confined. When those slaves gained the right to hold their own celebrations, they called the site where they met tango or tambo. There is evidence this word was in use for over two centuries. According to philologist Fernando Ortiz, tangu or tuñgu means dance in Central African languages. In the Río de la Plata area, official documents of the Spanish Viceroyalty used it in the early 19th century, ordering: "The dances known by the name of tangos are prohibited". For over a century, the word tango has been applied to the melodic-rhythmic invention, an extraordinarily original dance style, created in the metropolis of Buenos Aires on the Río de la Plata.

The rise of the tango between 1880 and 1890 was associated with two inseparable phenomena: the musical rhythms that already existed there and the mixing of *criollos* with the immigrant population packed into the urban outskirts of Buenos Aires and other cities like Montevideo and Rosario. It was created and developed distinct from the basic elements that originally served it.

In forming the musical and danceable genre called tango as a distinct entity, the next major influence had one foot in the European contradanza (Spanish) and the other in rhythm (African). You can certainly say tango was born as a new form from the habanera, milonga, Andalusian tango, and the candombe, popular styles in their own right at the dawning of the tango era.

It was *orillero* in origin, and never stopped being suburban in nature. The *orilla* (outskirts) of the city were the suburbs, of course, but so were the *conventillos* (a type of tenement building where poor people lived in crowded conditions). Some of those tenements were located just a few streets away from the city center. *Criollos, mestizos,* free blacks, and the substantial population of European immigrants coexisted there. The tango emerged from that ever-expanding mixture of races, origins, and destinies. A great number of its creators and lovers were rootless people brought together by the pressing needs of the moment. In bordellos, taverns, the courtyards of tenements, the dance became the key to coming together they could call their own. The tango was born joining heads and hearts, intertwining the legs in dance. Some imagined that its sequences of dance movements, sudden and primal, were inherited from ancient Egyptian and Greek dances, and they never lost some element of the ceremonial and sacred. Maybe they are the forms of a forgotten language we feel we're on the verge of figuring out when we dance.

It was invented by men and women who emerged from anonymity and the vast majority of them disappeared back into obscurity. It was the beginning of a period of incessant, non-stop improvisation, the work of characters who left behind this verse of their fame for us:

Cuando hago un doble corte
corre la voz por el Norte

si es que me encuentro en el Sur.[1]

The tango was invented for moving arm-in-arm, to become mutually self-absorbed and maintain the fascination in the eyes of onlookers. The tango was danced to build a fleeting image that would flow and remain fixed in the memories of spectators, fulfilling the desire to move and linger in place, defying indifference.

The tango's sensual nature and risque association with bordellos took it from the outskirts to reach the great capitals of Europe. Only after being accepted there was it welcomed in the center of the rioplatense capital cities. Some of the more overtly provocative dance steps and sequences had to be toned down for that to happen. It would be inaccurate to sketch out linear developments in the history of tango as a dance style. Its history includes moments of searching, stylization, developing the imaginary axis created by man and woman, generating an infinite number of ways for a couple to glide across the dance floor arm-in-arm.

The facts are there, as Jorge Luis Borges described:

Esa ráfaga, el tango, esa diablura,
los atareados años desafía;
Hecho de polvo y tiempo, el hombre dura
menos que la liviana melodía...[2]

In conjunction with the literary and journalistic uproar accompanying its first decades of existence, the tango sent shivers through church pulpits as a Spanish verse *(copla)* from that era illustrates:

---

[1] When I do a double cut/ word-of-mouth reaches the North/ even though I'm dancing in the South

[2] This gust, the tango, this devilish mischief/ the busy years challenge/ Made of dust and time, man endures/ less than the fleeting melody

Dicen que el tango es de una gran languidez
y que por eso lo prohibió Pío X.[3]

As the "fleeting melody" continued to develop in the 20th century this musical and danceable way of feeling, tango academies were proliferating, the fashion-tango, tea-tango, champagne tango... in London, New York, Paris, Rome, Madrid, Barcelona.

The musical invention

During its early decades, tango had the good fortune of being performed both by schooled musicians and self-taught musicians who played by ear. It grew up with the musical staff close at hand, and that gave its original purity an insurance policy for survival.

The primitive trios (guitar, violin and flute) and quartets (guitar, *bandoneón*, violin, and piano) were followed by the formidable strength of the orchestral ensemble. After that, tango was not solely the magnetic attraction of the rhythm that inspired dance steps and stares but a music that compelled audiences to sit down and listen spellbound. The great orquesta típica (bandoneones, full string section and piano) is its most fully evolved form even today.

The sound of the tango is pure, although not pure in origin. It emerged as an urban sound displaying elements of secular cosmopolitanism. How could it be anything else, if its point of reference was a broken heart, torn away from one land to take root in another, celebrating newness and nostalgia? From the outskirts of the city, the tango looked down wide boulevards towards the city center, where its followers spilled out into the streets,

---

[3] They say the tango comes from a great listlessness/ and that is why Pius X banned it

disrupting traffic.

It arrived via Corrientes Street, challenging the *cajetilla*[4]:

> *... Que no sabés del encanto*
> *de haber derramado llanto*
> *por un amor de mujer.*

> *Que decís que un tango "rante"*
> *no te hace perder la calma*
> *y que no te llora el alma*
> *cuando gime un bandoneón.*[5]

ESTEBAN CELEDONIO FLORES

Just a few years after it was created, the tango brazenly turned its attention towards Europe. It arrived there almost virginal, inexperienced, but with the credibility afforded by the portable organ, the *bandoneón*, the instrument it made its own to sing the liturgy of love in taverns and cabarets. Although the tango could be played with just one instrument, it has the power to fill a concert hall, equally at home before a numerous audience or an intimate private gathering. If it was originally a joyful, light-hearted music, it could no longer be that with the *bandoneón*. On the largest dance floors where it shares the space alongside jazz, cha-cha-cha, pasodoble and other rhythms, the tango always claims its place as the dance that dives most deeply into our nocturnal life, revolving around the question about who we are. Just as there are no conclusions in tango lyrics, there is no final closure to the dance. The possibilities for improvisation on the basic embrace are immeasurable.

Tango's evolution as a musical genre accompanied the

---

[4] *Cajetilla:* rich young man of the city, drawn to tango for thrills and excitement

[5] ...you don't know the beauty/ of having shed tears/ over the love of a woman
You say the tango "rante"/ does not move you/ and your soul does not cry/
when the bandoneon plays

tentative forays that modernity exhibited about our changing way of sensing the world. In short, its creativity sinks its roots deep into the most fundamental questions of contemporary life.

Mythical setting

The city of tango has changed. The one that appears visible today with the typical profile of modern anonymity is not anything like the earlier one that lingers on only in a few persistent pockets and a particular way of walking. That period of cosmopolitan upheaval is gone. The exploits of the *compadre* and *mina*[6], around whom the tango built its mythology, vanished. A peculiar achievement marked by doubts, bouts of indecision, disappointments, and pedestrian practices. However, with enough inspiration to know that sometimes love, hate, the passions, can't be induced. You don't love someone for whatever the other person grants you or means to you. You love them because you love them.

On another level, the tango repeats the offense by bringing it up again, because tragedy lies at the basic core of being. The intuitive poets of tango knew that our lives weave a path through the tangled web of the tragic (or comic, depending on how you look at it.) The tango unearths the force of destiny. The characters, revealed in all their nakedness, frequently exist in a state prior to forgiveness and remorse. Their passions, as in fairy tales or classic tragedy, border on the terrible and possess the keys to heaven and hell. From that perspective, to be upset by the emotional rawness of tango would be akin to being shocked by the cruelty of warriors in the classics. In that case, if there were grounds for outrage, our modern world wouldn't be familiar with the massive turnout for film noir movies, the epics of cowboys and aliens, or the series of

---

[6] *Compadre:* leader who earned respect for his own merits
Mina: woman

horror films.

Under its protection, the "fleeting melody" continues growing. Numerous fusions made it original and innovative. Finally, the tango would no longer be the exclusive province of stories of the suburban neighborhoods, *paicas,* outlaws, and *compadritos*[7]. They say that it was born universal and urban in nature, not just for a simple wordplay but because intimacy comes more frequently in the cities and has specific traits identifiable in any city in the world. The images of the tango project personal experiences in a language knowledgeable about the human heart and therefore are recognizable in distant lands.

Cuando estén secas las pilas
de todos los timbres que vos apretás.[8]
ENRIQUE SANTOS DISCÉPOLO

Farol...
las cosas que ahora se ven.
Farol...
ya no es lo mismo que ayer.[9]
HOMERO EXPÓSITO

... las calles y las lunas suburbanas
y tu amor en mi ventana
todo ha muerto, ya lo sé.[10]
HOMERO MANZI

---

[7] *Paica:* woman intimately involved in the tango world
Compadrito: "wannabe" compadre, a caricature of one

[8] When the batteries of all the bells/ you ring are worn out

[9] Streetlight.../ the things you are seeing now/ Streetlight.../ already are not the same as yesterday

[10] ...the suburban streets and moons/ and your love in my window/ It's all dead, I know that now.

The ephemeral legends of our modern cities fit there. They peer out at our individual realities, mixed and jumbled together, announcing that in some way we are all alike here, there and everywhere. Discovering that they, the tango dancers, found a destiny, a fact of life, as they often say. Something to give you a reason for living and a tradition where you can take refuge when it's time to die. No small thing amidst so much modern or South American disaffection. And finally it is reason to emphasize and magnify the importance of Carlos Gardel, who invented the style for turning those enigmas of life into song.

The voice of the tango: Carlos Gardel

Several decades after the tango was created, after its position as a dance and musical style was already consolidated, its voice appeared. The human voice that sounded like an orchestra arrived, harmonious and radical so the discovery of that dance of embrace would be complete. This was no lyrical poem which commented on the music with the proper expression, but the voice containing all the drama of a man's life, of a woman, within a single song. The voice of Carlos Gardel, capable of holding the attention of a packed theater by itself. When they put him with an orchestra, he warned the musicians: "You stick to the score, I'm the one who makes the melody." He began singing about love and being abandoned in love. But the themes of urban life soon entered the lyrics of the tango. Irony was introduced later, the metaphysical contempt. The listeners were the neighborhood, women, friends, those of us who were waiting for its dramatic account in some place in time. Neither the sublime nor the sordid could make the poets stay silent.

Carlos Gardel created a school that perhaps was the only one where tango singers went to be inspired. His phrase: "I make the melody" refers to the personal and exclusive requirement that

Berta Gardes, mother
of Carlos Gardel.

Gardel as a child

tango demands of every artist performing its drama in song. There were notable male singers who followed him, including Fiorentino, Rivero and Goyeneche... and among the female singers, Mercedes Simone, Nelly Omar, Libertad Lamarque, Rosanna Falasca, Virginia Luque... and many others. An unmistakable personal nuance is always present in the singing style of each one.

Carlos Gardel was not only a voice. He was also a style. Originally, he was just one more man among the thousands of poor immigrants who arrived along the Río de la Plata. Using the lessons gained in the open-door school of the street, and the rise to prominence prompted by his artistic successes, he blazed his own individual way of living a destiny. Hard-working and likable, a form of animal instinct --as they would say in the 19th century-- encouraged him to believe in the genius that marked his voice. Secure in that certainty perfected over the years, he continues

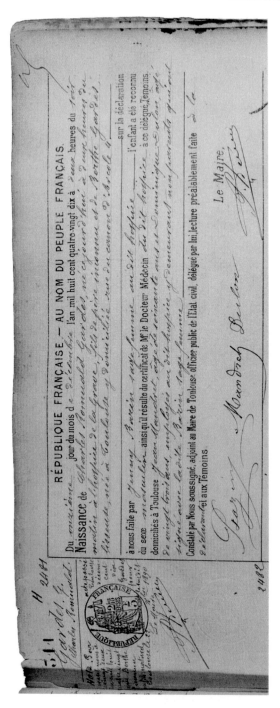

Birth Certificate of Charles Romuald Gardes, born in Toulouse, France.

singing his never-ending tango to us.

According to his birth certificate, Carlos Gardel was born at 2:00 a.m. on December 11, 1890 in St. Joseph de la Grave hospital in the city of Toulouse in southern France, located on the banks of the Garonne River. Before the expansion of the Roman Empire, it existed as a Gallic community. During the Middle Ages in Europe, it was an area with a strong Cathar influence that stimulated, via labyrinthine paths, the development of the poetry of the "gay science". In effect,

House where Carlos Gardes lived as a child, Toulouse.

music and lyrics joined together in a deeply aesthetic-philosophical sense in the works of these medieval troubadours.

His birth certificate declares he was the son of Berthe Gardes, clothes presser, living at Canón d´Arcole, 4, in her native city of Toulouse. No man acknowledged the newborn child as his son. Nor did the family of the single mother look favorably on the child in those years when marriage was such a deeply established institution. Berthe would ultimately decide to emigrate. But where? Most Europeans of that era went to the Americas, which had two notable centers for receiving and welcoming immigrants, the United States and Argentina. Berthe chose the south, Buenos Aires, and arrived at the port there aboard the steamship Don Pedro on March 11, 1893. She was leading her child Charles Romuald by the hand, along with a few pieces of luggage, her trade as a clothes presser, and her 27 years of age. She arrived with a person to contact, a fellow Frenchwoman named Mrs. Anais Breaux, who directed her to find lodging at 162 Uruguay Street and gave her work in her pressing shop.

Young Charles became Carlos or "Frenchy" in Buenos Aires, where everyone adapted and adopted the language and customs of the country. Even if the true school of his life was the street, it didn't prevent him from getting his primary school education, receiving a grade of "distinguished" even as his behavior was characterized by lack of discipline. Later his mother enrolled him in the arts and trades school so he would learn to make a living in a "useful occupation". He finished his studies when he was 14, his life already affected by his love for singing, an art he practiced in school choirs, on street corners and neighborhood taverns.

Craft and destiny of the singer

Towards the end of the 19th century, stanzas from the gaucho poem *Martín Fierro* were circulating in various circles of Argentinean popular art. The highly regarded epic poem ranks among the major works of the Spanish language heritage. Among those stanzas, one that was being constantly repeated confesses:

> *Cantando me he de morir*
> *cantando me han de enterrar*
> *y cantando he de llegar*
> *al pie del eterno Padre*
> *desde el vientre de mi madre*
> *vine a este mundo a cantar.*[11]

Perhaps those verses cannot be applied to anyone with greater justice than Carlos Gardel.

---

[11] Singing I will die/ Singing they will bury me/ And singing I will arrive/ at the feet of the eternal Father/ From my mother's womb/ I came into this world to sing

Apart from working different trades, he walked extensively around Buenos Aires and other cities in Argentina, as well as Montevideo. He was learning about lifestyles and ways of being that would later make it easy for him to embody numerous characters in "the great human comedy of a city" that is sung about in tangos. As he recalled in 1930, "I picked through trash looking for cardboard to salvage, worked as a watchmaker, a typesetter's apprentice". The concerns of his mother Berta (as she was known in Argentina) trying to track down the whereabouts of her rambling son, preoccupied with his passion for singing and how to earn a living with traditional occupations, are noted in many printed letters. She also mentioned his love for the intricacies of lyrical theaters and comedies. In 1936 Berta Gardes declared to *La Canción Moderna* magazine:

> "Since we were living across from the Teatro Politeama, and I worked for some famous people, he frequently went into the dressing rooms, where everyone really loved him. He had listened to some operas and sang them afterwards since he had a good ear, playing all the roles himself..."

He learned some of the tools of the lyrical tradition trade there, from vocal projection and diction to different embellishments developed by the operatic school. A tradition that undoubtedly sinks its roots in the remote discoveries of troubadours from Toulouse. He himself said that his attempts to sing a la Caruso or Tita Ruffo then were famous.

But the tango would not be what it is if it had lacked the wealth of emotions and singing styles contributed by the criollo song tradition, from which Gardel drew on and performed over his entire career. *Estilos, tonadas, cifras, zambas, vidalitas,* all combined to form a collection of material that grew continually through the work of *payadores* and popular musicians. They requested those songs in the taverns, along with the ones Gardel was identified with as a singer of previously composed pieces, as

Gardel as a young man
in the neighborhood of Abasto in Buenos Aires.

opposed to the art of the *payadores* who improvised the verses in the moment of the performance.

Interim (1904-1910)

For a period of some six years, from 1904-1910, the life of the future great singer passed into the shadows. There is no known record of what happened in his life supported by corroborating documentation. His mother stated Gardel went away with a friend to Montevideo and she had no news of him for years. The allure of the unknown during this period creates an extra enigmatic power to Gardel's personality that links him to other historical figures who were on the brink of achieving legendary status. In my opinion, the onstage game of turning into someone else, leaving conventional language behind and to come in performing, acting just like anyone else in different environments and codes of life, represents the great fortune of the tango-song, enabling it to reach its consummate level of artistic expression. It is a theatrical interpretation that rose out of certain lessons learned that will turn out to be more creative the more intimate and committed they are.

But he wasn't completely absent from Buenos Aires. Some accounts place him there singing and accompanying himself on guitar. His friend Esteban Capot, another Frenchman, was the person who helped him with his first tentative strums on the instrument, by Capot's own account. The young man was preparing himself in the art and crucial command of the language customs of the great port city which, at times, doubled its native population with the arrival of substantial numbers of overseas immigrants. One day, the prodigal son returned home and his mother (single, although she would call herself a widow to avoid insults) welcomed him warmly. The son would never abandon his desire to roam the streets but he would not make his mother suffer through such an extended absence again.

Gardel as a young man, sporting the kind of gaucho outfit
he wore when he sang folk songs.

Morocho and Zorzal in a young country (1910)

Argentina celebrates 100 years as an independent nation in 1910. The figures of economic prosperity are extraordinary. Paradoxically, it appears like an illusion to any rational mind when compared to the country's rank in the world today. Then the railway lines stretched out to the deepest parts of *La Pampa*. They built grain silos, cold-storages, expanded the ports, and created the modern profile of the city. Hundreds of thousands of immigrants were pouring in, because people emigrate to those places on the planet where the possibility exists for them to prosper. The centennial was commemorated just like the great celebration that greeted the dawning of the 20th century. Both native Argentineans and the recent arrivals were becoming aware of their identity. It is true they were divided by social class, with landowners and the bourgeoisie facing the proletariat. The *Federación Obrera* (Worker's Federation) had organized a protest march with 100,000 people in the street, close to ten per cent of the population. In politics, the confrontation was between conservatives and radicals, the latter movement including a thriving middle class on the rise. Another, more subtle division affected the taste of the era to an equal degree, pitting intellectuals, politicians and the classic ruling elite who despised and looked down on tango against the people from the outskirts and the noisy, boisterous city who lived it with unrestrained enthusiasm.

The tracks of Carlos Gardel (still Gardes at this point) become more visible starting in 1910. He was now a well-known singer in the neighborhood surrounding the Mercado de Abasto. His presence brightened the neighborhood courtyards, where he was surrounded by youthful admirers who listened raptly as if they perceived in Gardel a prodigy who could project their own dreams and desires.

His appearance at Café O'Rodeman managed by the Traverso brothers, notorious brawlers and hard-core right wingers, was much commented on and widely related. But there are also accounts of performances at meetings of the opposing political camp. If we look at what he sang throughout his career, trying to see if the songs he chose tell us something about the man, there are radically contradictory indications when it comes to politics. From a broader perspective, the tango in fact has always had an aroma of the suburbs, of that *orillero* origin so well described by Gardel in the tango *Melodía de Arrabal.*

He was nicknamed the *Morocho del Abasto*[12] from the neighborhood where he first gained renown, and also the *Zorzal*[13], alluding to the elegant songbird so beloved in the Argentinean countryside. In fact, his relationships with cowboys, slaughterhouse butchers, and stall holders from the meat markets of Buenos Aires would help him to make a name for himself in the *criollo* song tradition. He took part in traditional circles that extolled the virtues of the gaucho legacy. Similarly, the substantial number of Italian immigrants introduced the *canzonettas* to Argentina, another favorite style of Gardel for many years. The influence of the lyric opera tradition, for which Gardel felt a special and ongoing admiration, persisted alongside these other musical currents. Argentina was on the map as a destination for opera singers traveling from Europe in search of large audiences and hefty paychecks. The flagship theater in the Americas for this art form, the *Teatro Colón*, enjoyed a singular prestige since its inauguration in 1908 and continued to be a venue of major importance.

The singers meet (1911)

The reputation of the *Morocho del Abasto* grew both inside and outside his home territory. Along with musicians and singers they claimed as their own, some neighborhoods would later champion a

---

[12] *Morocho:* person with dark brown or black hair
[13] *Zorzal:* thrush

group of young dancers who represented a particular style or way of performing in the tango dance halls. The reputation of Carlos Gardel reached Balvanera Sur, the neighborhood that boasted its own singer in José Razzano. Born in Montevideo, Razzano was also pursuing a career in Buenos Aires as a singer of folk and traditional songs. His center of activity was the Café del Pelado (at the corner of Entre Ríos and Moreno), where they encouraged him to go find (bump into, they said) the *Morocho* in *Abasto*. A house on Guardia Vieja street owned by a pianist named Gijena served as the setting. Approximately 30 people attended the session between the two singers. First one sang, then the other, and afterwards they sang together as a duo until the early morning hours. It was habitual among the *payadores* (folk singers and improvising poets who sang accompanying themselves on guitar) to suggest a competition in the form of a tournament where a winner would be declared. But in the case that concerns us, the singers weren't improvising, but singing songs with already established lyrics and music. The results were heartily cheered by the audience and the foundation for a relationship between the artists was put in place that night that would have major implications for their future. After some time passed, it would be Gardel who returned the visit to Razzano's home turf. Once again, a packed crowd enthusiastically applauded their performance. Between the cheers and some time spent thinking it over, the idea emerged of forming a duo to tour around Buenos Aires province, although the proposed duo would in fact become a trio after another singer, Francisco Martino, joined them.

First recordings and tours (1912-1914)

Before hitting the road, Carlos Gardel signed a contract with the Columbia label on April 2, 1912 to make his first recordings. The contract specified that it was made between "the agent for Columbia, José Tagini and Mr. Carlos Gardel, a national singer by profession, writer of verses and prose, and improviser of popular music". The contract stipulated the singer would record fifteen sides and be paid 180 pesos. In the end, fourteen songs were released with a label reading, "Carlos Gardel, tenor with guitar". Critic Rubén Pesce, after analyzing the emotional expressiveness of Gardel's voice, comments, "his school is a combination of the popular bards of particular taste with the theatrical singers he often imitated".

Those first discs have been re-issued frequently and enable listeners today to have some idea of the extraordinary artist he was going to become.

José Razzano ultimately didn't take part in that first planned tour. Gardel and Martino did it by themselves, earning very little money but gaining a wealth of valuable professional experience.

Once the duo returned to Buenos Aires, the trio re-formed with Razzano and later became a quartet with the addition of an experienced singer and composer, Saúl Salinas. They started another tour that also failed to make much money. During that tour, first Salinas and later Martino left the group. The Gardel-Razzano duo came back to Buenos Aires after a few months with a wealth of performances under their belts, no money in their pockets and very uncertain prospects for the future.

A historical resource of interest is the curious purchase of a 48-page notebook by Carlos Gardel to paste in the newspaper clippings that mentioned his performances. He named it "Chronicle of My Artistic Tour". One clip from the *El Censor* daily paper of Bragado in Buenos Aires province dated September 17, 1913 reads:

"The *criollo trio* of Gardes-Martino and Razzano will make their debut in the Teatro Francés tonight. These three *criollos* sing all kinds of national tunes accompanied by vihuela and arrive with a reputation for being quite good, according to reviews from the venues where they previously performed. They are not *payadores* but rather singers who give voice to select poetic fragments that are emotional, philosophical or humorous, refined and pleasing: We recommend that people turn out to hear these three *criollos* whose performances will brighten the Teatro Francés today and tomorrow and are professional singers for the Columbia and Victor labels". (Gardel for Columbia and Razzano on Victor).

Back in Buenos Aires again, as a tango from the 1940s says, waiting for the elusive opportunity that would come... or not. The days went by without a single significant job appearing. Then Pancho Taurel, an influential resident of the city, called his friend José Razzano one day to provide entertainment for a nighttime party at the *Confitería Perú*. Razzano showed up with Gardel and together they brought energy and spirit to an evening that continued in a bordello and extended even longer at the most famous cabaret of the era, the Armenonville. It was the spot where the so-called golden youth (golden from money and occasionally from fame) gathered to hang out. The duo's songs thrilled the audience. The impact was so powerful the cabaret owners decided on the spot to offer them daily performances for a fantastic fee (70 pesos of that era), starting the very next night in December 1913.

That was the day that ultimately opened the doors to the general public for the Gardel-Razzano duo. On January 08, 1914, they were already performing at the Teatro Nacional, the start of a brilliant career that took them through theaters, cinemas and finally the recording studios of Buenos Aires.

When they performed at the Armenonville cabaret, they always sang the *criollo* folk songs together. We would say that a repertoire was expanding there, the *canción nacional* (national song), and the Gardel-Razzano duo was instrumental in contributing to that process. Who performed there? No less than the best tango orchestras, like the one led by Roberto Firpo, whose line-up at that time included the *Tigre del Bandoneón*, Eduardo Arolas, and violinist Tito Rocatagliata.

Certainly Argentina, celebrated as a young, independent nation in 1910, could congratulate itself for boasting such an exquisite popular art of its own.

Carlos Gardel and Jose Razzano formed the best duo
in Argentina for over ten years.

That eventful, partly impromptu performance at the
Armenonville triggered the duo's live introduction into theaters.
The press of the era reported:

> "In the intermission, Mr. Gardel and Mr. Razzano made the
> audience applaud enthusiastically by singing *criollo* styles and
> accompanying themselves on guitar".

2. THE GREAT LEAP (1914-1923)

Their live appearances were not confined solely to Buenos Aires. The major cities in the interior of Argentina (Córdoba and Rosario) also featured the duo as an attraction during theater intermissions. This is a good time to point out that this receptive environment was created by the gifted stars of the *rioplatense* theater scene: Florencio Parravicini, Lola Membrives, Roberto Casaux, etc.

The fact that songs from the folk tradition continued to share the same stages with the dance and music of the tango only obeyed a natural logic. It took place in other cabarets after the Armenonville, and in theaters where the danced tango had the good fortune of crossing over as both a dance and scenic illustration dating from the end of the 19th century. However, it was as if the word was still held hostage by the *criollo* song tradition. The tango was played by the orchestras in the cabarets and theaters, and danced on the dance floors... The national singers performed so that the audience in concert halls would listen in their seats. What were they singing about? Narrative tales and images drawn from the rich rural tradition. The tango still had no lyrics, which means: the city applauded and shook with excitement over the criollo song but still had not discovered the way of singing its own reality.

Carlos Gardel always cultivated close relations with the tango musicians and dancers, as well as the theater actors who danced it onstage. Among them was a renowned professional, José Ovidio Bianquet, *El Cachafaz*, director of the most popular academy for learning to dance the tango. Gardel shared his passion for the dance and, during one performance in Chile as part of the renowned Gardel-Razzano duo, he spiced up the performance by dancing the tango.

In 1915, a serious incident started at the door of the Palais de Glace cabaret and moved into the nearby streets. It ended with a shot that wounded Gardel in his left chest. According to newspaper accounts, he had gone outside in defense of his friend, actor Elías Alippi. Apparently, there were ulterior motives in play for the attacker, who snapped at Gardel: "Now you're not going to sing 'El Moro' anymore". The incident did not have serious after-effects, although Gardel carried the bullet lodged in his left lung for the rest of his life.

That year was one for consolidation of the artistic ground gained and a higher profile in neighboring countries: Uruguay and Brazil. In their trip to the latter, they happened to meet the great tenor Enrico Caruso, who sang for the duo in private and gave Gardel some advice:

> "You have a beautiful voice, a great one. Don't be seduced by easy successes or false experts. Reject any suggestions anyone might make about changing so you can reach one or two extra notes that are higher than your natural range. If you do that, it will ruin your voice. In addition to your voice, you have an unmistakable gift: very pure diction, it's clear, perfect. That is very valuable. It will enable you to accurately introduce any note in the proper pitch".

At the time, the popular audiences, intellectual circles and political leaders (the latter two being tightly linked) recognized the duo as representative of a modern form Argentina could call its own. That's why they were summoned on August 18, 1916 to provide the color of national music at the reception for the visiting Spanish writers Ortega y Gasset, Ortega Munilla and Santiago Rusiñol.

The economic situation had improved markedly for both men. Gardel moved into a better house at 1714 Corrientes Street with his mother. They regularly shared bills with the most important foreign actors and actresses who visited Argentina and simultaneously linked their careers to the dynamic *criollo* theater world that was producing a steady stream of plays. There was no shortage of opportunities to attend the opera theaters, either. Razzano relates that on the night they went to the *Teatro Colón* to listen to the *bel canto* of tenor Giovanni Martinelli, Gardel exclaimed when they returned to his house:

- "You saw Pepe? Gold nuggets come out of that throat!"

Before 1917, a crucial year for both Gardel and tango in general, the Gardel-Razzano duo became a trio of guitars with the addition of José Ricardo, an extraordinary intuitive musician who would play a notable role for many years as Gardel's career flourished. His musical prowess began to stand out when Gardel chose to feature his unaccompanied singing on several songs drawn from the folk tradition like *El Moro, El Pangaré, Lo que Fui, Amargura* and others. A path where Gardel's leading role converged with the support of strings provided by the stimulating presence of José Ricardo.

Contursi-Gardel (1916-1917)

Since its birth sometime between 1880 and 1890 (those are approximate but not exact dates), the tango was a popular phenomenon that had consolidated its status as a dance and music by the first decade of the 20th century. It made the journey from the outskirts to the capital cities of Europe and the city center of Buenos Aires, which eventually accepted it as a product of authentic *rioplatense* originality. It brought its suburban identity and aromas of the land with it, where La Pampa could be glimpsed at the end of the fervent city streets. There any number of musical pieces that recalled oxen, wagons, winds, dirt roads, and outdoor landscapes. An immense rural horizon that already had its song and essential poetry written in what was called gaucho poetry. The city had the tango to call its own, but still had not found its epiphany in the song. Rough lyrics boast about the characters to the tune of a *cuplé*, or compositions of tentative declarations like *La Morocha* by Villoldo represented attempts that were still too timid, premature. It was between 1915 and 1917 when a popular singer and lyric writer named Pascual Contursi began to give shape to what would be the thematic premise of the lyrics. Working with surprising intuition, he provided the tango with the blueprint of a world, or one suggested in the phrasing. From beginning to end of the poem, there are verses rich in content, sometimes of being overwhelmed by feeling, with suggestive entrances and exits. Making use of the music from previously acclaimed tangos, Contursi decided to tell a story in his piece using language that reflected the way people talked in the street. In 1916, he composed the lyric that relates a personal story of being left by a lover, adapted to the music of the tango "Lita", written by Samuel Castriota. Contursi had been trying to write theater pieces since he was a young boy, and here he achieved the essential dramatic tension that the tango-song will display in its brief, three-minute duration. Gardel learned the lyric and applied his own vocal flair to it in order to sing the song for his circle of friends. It took some time before he dared to sing it in public. That happened during a performance in mid-1917 at the famous Teatro Empire in Buenos Aires, where the Gardel-Razzano duo was accompanied by guitarist José Ricardo. He sang it solo there, as he would sing the lengthy list of tangos that were taking their definitive form from

Carlos Gardel, José Ricardo and José Razzano in 1917.
Ricardo was the first guitarist of the group.

that point on, creating the performance style for them that has endured to this day. Apparently, his duo colleague didn't consider it appropriate to include a song in tango tempo in the repertoire. As we mentioned before, until that point the duo had performed pieces from the folk songbook, whose verses were built in the mold of *gauchesca* poetry or conventional popular language. Contursi's lyric to the tango "Lita", which Gardel re-named *Mi Noche Triste* (My Sorrowful Night), started up with all the considerable power of the genre while its words drew from *lunfardo* expressions excluded from the *criollo* songbook. They were voices created on the outskirts of Buenos Aires, that molten suburban magma that mixed together people recently arrived via the port with the natives, eager to tell of the things that went on there in vividly colorful detail using the language exclusively from those areas. The words of the first line, *Percanta que me amuraste* would naturally be understood by the people living on the outskirts but not the "good people" in the major cities along the Rio de la Plata.

Two developments occurred that year that added special impact to the powerful turn of events working in favor of Gardel's artistic destiny. The first was having a major role as an actor in the silent film *Flor de Durazno*, based on a famous novel of the same name written by the successful author Hugo Wast. Although Gardel viewed himself as too fat and clumsy as an actor, the film producers managed to persuade him to finish filming by promising that he would appear performing with his guitar. The lead actress, Ilda Pirovano, related that he chased after her, asking her to teach him some Italian *canzonettas*. They also remember the good-natured humor characteristic of his personality throughout his entire life. He made an unwavering commitment to work on his body through physical exercise and badly managed diets, until he finally managed to reduce his weight from the 118 kilos (260 pounds) he weighed then to 76 kilos (167 pounds) in 1932. A real prodigious feat of willpower, rewarded, of course, by the success his presence achieved on theater stages and movie screens.

On tour from Buenos Aires out towards the other Argentinean provinces almost constantly during 1917, the duo arrived at Mendoza and from there moved on to Chile. In one of several performances there, at the *Teatro Olimpo* in Viña del Mar, Carlos Gardel danced the tango *Montevideo* with the Chilean singer Roxana. In the book 'Life of Carlos Gardel', Razzano remembered the incident as "an entertaining, spur-of-the-moment inspiration of Roxana and Carlos. He was a great tango dancer, of course, but never thought of putting his feet in serious competition with his marvelous voice." He would return to performing as a dancer in 1934 and 1935, this time in front of the movie cameras in the films *Cuesta Abajo* and *Tango Bar.*

The tango song (1917-1919)

The appearance of *Mi Noche Triste*, considered today to be the first sung tango, marked a fundamental shift in the history of the tango. Gardel recorded it for the *Odeón Nacional* label that same year of 1917 and Robert Firpo did an instrumental version with his Orchestra. In 1918, the Muiño and Alippi company included it as a song in the play *Los Dientes del Perro*, where it was sung by actress Manolita Poli during a run of over five hundred performances. The audience left the theater singing the verses they had just learned. From a repertoire of songs that reflected transformations of different natures, most of them referencing rural or country environments, now some verses were appearing with tango-derived music that were set in the environment where the tango first emerged: the city. The setting for the song is minimal, plain, and intimate: a room or place for romantic trysts *(cotorro)* where the male protagonist laments being left by his female lover.

Percanta que me amuraste
en lo mejor de mi vida
dejándome el alma herida
y esplín en el corazón.[14]

In a time when she knew she was loved, in a love that joined together joy and passion:

Sabiendo que te quería
que vos eras mi alegría
y mi sueño abrasador.[15]

What can happen for the protagonist, devastated in that room where wealth is measured by the magnetic force of the soul in love? Facing this abandonment, he will search out the company of alcohol that fakes providing him with an elixir for forgetting...

---

[14] Woman, you dumped me/ in the prime of my life/ Leaving my soul wounded/ and the blues in my heart.
[15] Knowing that I loved you/ That you were my joy/ and my burning love.

Y por eso me encurdelo
pa' olvidarme de tu amor. [16]

The days go by and she doesn't return. The things in the
cotorro where they shared their love betray her absence. Every
time the protagonist (guitarist and singer) returns there, he misses
the woman.

Cuando voy a mi cotorro
lo veo desarreglado,
todo triste, abandonado,
me dan ganas de llorar,
me detengo largo rato
campaneando tu retrato
pa' poderme consolar. [17]

The only thing he has to console himself with is a photograph
of her. He looks at it longingly, caught between the sadness and the
alcohol. When he goes to bed later, he leaves the door halfway
open in case she comes back.

De noche, cuando me acuesto,
no puedo cerrar la puerta,
porque dejándola abierta
me hago ilusión que volvés. [18]

Persisting in his hope, he confesses:

---

[16] That's why I'm getting drunk/ to forget about your love.

[17] When I return to my room/ I find it all messed up/ very sad, abandoned/ It makes me feel like crying/ and I spend long hours/ staring at your portrait/ to find solace.

[18] At night when I go to bed/ I can't close the door/ Because leaving it open/ I make believe that you're back.

Siempre traigo bizcochitos
pa' tomar con matecitos
como cuando estabas vos... [19]

At night, when he tries to sleep in the bed they shared, the *catrera,* it *se pone cabrera / porque no nos ve a los dos* (gets upset/because it doesn't see the two of us). The metaphor returns to insomnia, of tossing and turning, making the bedsprings squeak from the sense of helplessness caused by her absence.

Y si vieras la catrera
cómo se pone cabrera
cuando no nos ve a los dos. [20]

The woman's touch has unmistakably marked the room. The bottles are all decorated with *moñitos / todos de un mismo color* (little ribbons/ of the same color). The difficult use of the affectionate diminutives skillfully serves as counterpoint to the barren portrait painted of the room. The handful of objects there are in tune with the man's sorrow:

Ya no hay en el bulín
aquellos lindos frasquitos
adornados con moñitos
todos de un mismo color;
y el espejo está empañado
si parece que ha llorado
por la ausencia de tu amor. [21]

---

[19] I always bring cookies/ to drink with our little mates/ just like when you were here.

[20] And if you could see the bed/ how upset it becomes/ when it doesn't see the two of us.

[21] Now the *bulín* (room, apartment) does not have/ those pretty little bottles/ decorated with little ribbons/ all of the same color/And the mirror looks foggy/ it seems that it has cried/ over the absence of your love.

It is well known of lyrical poetry that you sing in order not to cry, or that the song is a form of sublimating the sadness, maybe even one of the ulterior motives behind the poetry. Nevertheless, in this tango:

La guitarra en el ropero
todavía está colgada:
nadie en ella canta nada
ni hace sus cuerdas vibrar... [22]

And the lamp doesn't want to light up either:

Y la lámpara del cuarto
también tu ausencia ha sentido
porque su luz no ha querido
mi noche triste alumbrar. [23]

It is a magnificent finale to the listing of facts described through actions. The abandonment concludes in silence and darkness that, albeit total, on the other hand is not definitive. It shares a situation, a dark night in the room and in the soul of the protagonist. We've learned what the lover was like through the exquisite tenderness and affection shown for the things that formed the scenic backdrop of that love. Far from the customary hard feelings that years later will shape the black myth about tango lyrics, the man isn't furious, or jealous, or harboring thoughts of revenge in his heart. Instead there is hope, sadness over her absence, and desire to restore the lost relationship.

Pascual Contursi undoubtedly knew the story he wrote quite well. Shortly after triumphing with the lyrics for tangos, he tried

---

[22] The guitar in the closet/ is still hanging/ Nobody ever sings anything/ or makes its strings vibrate...

[23] And the lamp in the room/ has also felt your absence/ because its light has not wanted/ to light up my sorrowful night

his luck at *sainetes* (humorous theatrical dramas in one act) with excellent and lucrative results. The following year, prior to anyone else, he offered him an excellent new sung tango, *Flor de Fango*, that Gardel recorded in 1919.

The changes in Carlos Gardel's career were beginning to become evident. Not just for the revolutionary innovation of introducing tangos into the repertoire but also in the increasing number of solo performances of folk songs. The records were selling quickly and constantly. They were recorded using the acoustic system where the singer performed in front of a large horn that transmitted the vibrations of the voice to the wax master.

Magazines, posters, and music scores were regularly spreading the word of the existence and work of the duo. Their performing innovations had created a new form that injected fresh life into theater intermissions, interludes in film screenings, and appearances at public events. Both the press and record industry publicity hailed the greater prominence being earned by folk music with a strong national flavor, in those times when the waves of immigrants were diversifying the criollo customs and traditions with additions from their own native cultures. The concern of the ruling classes focused on defusing the effect of egalitarian ideas advocated by labor spokesmen, most of whom were immigrants themselves. Many of those ideas, in the form of demands for social recognition and an indictment of the capitalist state, had convinced thousands of organized workers in leftist labor unions. In 1919, when the democratic government was still led by the middle classes, there would an impressive movement for recognition that resulted in clashes with the police over an entire week. These blood-drenched days were subsequently named the "Tragic Week" for the more than 70 people who lost their lives during the ensuing repression.

Maturing over time

There is a tendency to point to one year, 1917, and a single performance that year, Gardel singing *Mi Noche Triste* in the Teatro Empire, as the start of the chain of events that resulted in the tango-song. The extraordinary results include such songs as *Malevaje, Mano a Mano, Al Mundo le Falta un Tornillo, Melodía de Arrabal, Confesión,* and *Yira-Yira.* Later came *Cambalache, Sur, Malena, Percal, Como Dos Extraños* and a lengthy etc. Some people suggest that the tango-song was created fully formed, when Gardel first sang it in public in Buenos Aires on the date mentioned above.

We can listen to the version of *Mi Noche Triste* that Gardel recorded in 1917 and compare it with the second version he recorded in 1930, or other tangos he recorded starting in 1926. The evidence from these tests is irrefutable. The artist traveled an arduous, uphill trail. The first obstacle he had to overcome was resistance to tangos being sung that way. His partner Razzano was also reluctant, although he later acted as an effective supplier of tangos for Gardel and even wrote the lyrics to some songs. There weren't many songs in that vein in their early days, and the duo also had to give them their definitive form so they would sound better as tangos. Gardel was very prone to introducing changes. That can be confirmed by comparing the music and lyrics written by other songwriters with the recordings that Gardel made of them. Several studies have pointed out the skill and sharp instincts he had for changing words or phrases written by authors who were notably more literate.

From the above, one can be sure that he was a *criollo* singer then and identified as such by his audience. He himself was convinced of the relevance of the full thematic range included in that genre for his voice. In turn, he drew on the *criollo-folklórico* song for his repertoire up to the final phase of his career. Similarly, until the final stages of the 1910s and start of the 1920s, Carlos Gardel was considered a national singer, since he was frequently labeled that in his duo appearances with Razzano. He still was not identified as a singer of tangos. He was making his way along a very narrow trail he had opened and became the principal avenue for this music in about 10 years.

If we re-examine the recordings, the most direct form we have for appreciating how Gardel sang, we see that among the 66 songs recorded by the duo between 1917 and 1920, there is evidence of only eight tangos, all performed by Gardel solo. In 1922, eight tangos were also recorded. From then on, he moved ahead in a geometric progression until he turned into a singer of tangos, first and foremost, above and beyond any other category, sometime around 1924.

After the first tango sung by Gardel in 1917, men and women appeared right away with recordings that bear serious consideration. However, none had his ability or desire for self-improvement nor the number of songs to perform that he had available to him, apart from any specific evaluation of their talent as performers.

Setting the stage between 1917 and 1924

There are plenty of photographs from this era that show him as heavy. In 1921, he joined the gymnasium of the Young Men's Christian Association (YMCA), where witnesses and biographers agree in describing how Gardel subjected himself to grueling hours of daily workouts at the gym, wrapped in layers of rubber to stimulate perspiration. He did exercises used in training boxers and received "very hard massages for weight loss". He was gradually managing to reduce his weight in a tough, ongoing battle between his love for good food and the demands of the stage. They told him that physical exercise helped to keep the voice healthy, in addition to making his body trim, and he enthusiastically threw himself into the training. Several anecdotes point to his reluctance to stay up all night in situations just before performances. We suspect that those tales, whether true or apocryphal, spoke to his professionalism and truthfully are highly indicative of the sense of responsibility he felt for his body and voice.

Along with his fondness for good food, which didn't exclude some simple, tasty *criollo* dishes (as he sings in the tango *Seguí Mi Consejo: Morfate tus pucheretes en el viejo "Tropezón"*[24], a very popular Buenos Aires restaurant), he liked to dress in fine clothes, in some cases bordering on excess. In a certain sense, you could say he created styles or confirmed elegant habits that marked the most striking trends of the era. Hat, his hair always slicked back, suits in coordinated combination with shirts, ties, belts and shoes, always appropriate for every hour of the day and season of the year.

His reputation for coming to the aid of friends who were in trouble or down on their luck is famous. Gardel always generously made available the money he had already begun to earn with his art. He helped out and spent money on parties and at the racetracks, according to what he sings in several tangos.

His artistic preparation was not just limited to rehearsals and the search for new horizons crowned by the invention of the tango-song. Starting in 1918, he periodically received singing lessons from Eduardo Bonesi, who declared after analyzing Gardel's voice:

"He had a brilliant baritone register and was never off key. As for his *tessitura*, his range reached a full two octaves that he handled and controlled to full satisfaction. It's a good range for a popular singer. [...]. He was studious and responsible. He knew he was unique, one-of-a-kind in the genre and took care of his voice. Aware that you also take care of the voice through physical exercise, he did daily workouts at the gymnasium lasting for an hour or longer".

---

[24] Eat your stews at the old Tropezón

Dressed in gaucho stage attire with his guitar.
Studio photo.

The *El Día* daily newspaper in Montevideo wrote:

> "Carlitos spent the entire day singing, because he was a man who
> sang for the audience, true, but also for himself. It was something that
> came from his soul. When he finished running through the repertoire,
> you would frequently hear a Sagi Barba or Tito Schipa imitated to
> perfection".

It was proposed to him to perform those imitations on stage but
Gardel, respectful of his art, always opposed it.

From 1924 on, Carlos Gardel would be the tango singer par
excellence. He invented for himself a recognized destination, a
profession, and elicited an extraordinary interest in very
widespread audiences. And as opposed to the norm in earlier eras,
now it was the tango singer who also performed criollo folk songs.
At the same time he had transformed the tango. The first change
shifted the tempo from 2/4 to 4/8, and sometimes 4/4. In turn, in the
composition *Milonguita*, Enrique Delfino used the ABAB pattern
for the structure of the sung tango. A first part (A), a chorus (B), a
second part different from the first (A) followed by the same
refrain (B). In 1920 or 1921, Gardel gave the song the definitive
performance based on the arrangement conceived by Delfino.
Around the same dates he composed *Medallita de la Suerte* with
Razzano, a tango that Roberto Firpo's orchestra performed as an
instrumental. Gardel recorded it much later, in 1933.

People have said of the tango-song that it is a miniature
dramatic play with all its elements: presentation, development,
and denouement. The unadorned, stripped-down means for
representing it are the vocal inflections that tell the tale in song
accompanied by a defined musical arrangement. That way the
singer, by means of subtle and very understated movements,
generally facial, can convey dramatic changes that are
overflowing in the content of the words he sings. Perhaps the great
force of the Gardelian innovation lies in that very element: to
express with his vocal shadings the tremendous shifts in the lives

of characters whose entire existence occurs in the two or three minutes that the musical piece lasts.

Looking at it in greater depth, you realize right away that Gardel outdid himself and became a different artist at the beginning of the 1920s. His artistry took a giant leap to a higher level, one that determined his indisputable, enduring validity in time as a shining light that never loses its luster with the passing decades and certainly brought life and extremely valuable works to the tango-song arena. Once Gardel finished up his tuneful creation, he initiated the trans-Atlantic voyages with a tour of Spain to perform during the intermissions of theater plays. He was still accompanied by Razzano. If you listen to the recordings from those years, when the tangos performed solo are more prevalent than any other genre, you can clearly make out that the singer is already the master of his craft.

What did the lyrics express?

The tango is the song of affirmation by those characters who found their voice in this style, and simultaneously a mirror to reflect their lives. The cabarets, the jobs, the outbursts, the oversights, the desire to get away from or return to who you are, loves and hates, hopes, the deepest contempt and loyalties, the spoils of the soul, acknowledgment of foreign roots (mostly Italian and Spanish) are the subjects of its lyrics. Sometimes the tango itself is the subject of the lyric.

Conventional wisdom holds that Gardel was familiar with and listened to an average of 50 tangos, including *Volver, Caminito, Compadrón, Lo Han Visto con Otra, La Cumparsita, Yira-Yira...* However, not even multiplying that number by 10 would enable us to reach the full total of Gardel's work. But the qualitative is of far more interest to us here than the quantitative. During that decade of affirmation of the tango lyricist, the singer chose songs in which the dancers found a familiar world in the song. It was sung as a narrative that commented on stories that had emerged from a well-known environment and atmosphere, even philosophical reflections that later formed part of the commonplace sayings and expressions that popped up in daily conversation. *Sé poeta, incluso en prosa. Gran estilo (nada más bello que el lugar común)*[25], Baudelaire had advised. To create commonplace expressions that someone else could recognize and claim as their own surely is the highest aspiration of a poet.

It is helpful to point out that other voices appeared on the tango scene during that period, the actresses and actors singing in theater plays featuring tangos on stage.

In the 1920s, tango lyrics burst into view on the horizon of the song with dignity and grace, as if the faucet of popular poetry had suddenly been opened. It is ignorance, or bad faith, to indulge in simple reductionism like those who insist that the lament of the lover left behind, or the hoodlum's bravado, are the exclusive themes of the tango-song. Maybe the most striking and relevant constant is that so many of the lyrics tell tales that take place in the *milongas* or *bailongos* (dance halls). On the other hand, they frequently refer to themes very different from the one offered by Borges in *El Hombre de la Esquina Rosada* (The Man from the Pink Corner). The main female characters aren't always the desired *Lujaneras*, who normally end up with the toughest brawler from the outskirts. There are occasions, for example in the tango *La Milonga* by Cárdenas and Rossi, in which ...*la muchacha que al guapo adoró / Maldice al malevo que a su hombre mató.*[26]

Gardel lent his voice to the extraordinary abundance of compositions, represented the transformations they contained. Depending on the circumstances, his vocals included everything from lines drawn from the play to snippets of dialogue and

---

[25] Always be a poet, even in prose/ A great style (there is nothing more beautiful than a commonplace expression)

[26] ...the girl that the brave guy worshipped/ curses the outlaw who killed her man.

interjections that enriched the drama of the story being portrayed. Indeed, we can imagine that the tango, the musical and danceable event of that golden era, recognized its own scenarios in the singer's work. That's why most of the audience that applauded Gardel was made up of people who were habitually in attendance at the milongas, cabarets, and cafes that had a stage for orchestras.

Native of one country, Citizen with documents

The confused status of Carlos Gardel and his identity documents have been the subject of a great deal of literature, much of it controversial. At the end of the 19th century and start of the 20th, Argentina was a country which employed promotional campaigns in Europe to attract immigrants. When they arrived in the country, they declared their place of origin and, at the time they were issued documents certifying their identity, the names and surnames were altered on many occasions. Curious situations existed, like those of citizens from Arab-speaking (and writing) countries, when the conversion to Spanish names meant a complete change from their past identities. Later the obligations to the State continued in clarifying the status of the individuals or had the opposite effect of creating long-running conflicts that dragged on forever. But the standard outcome was that any irregularities were easily corrected.

There is no record of what documents Gardel used during his childhood and youth. Scholastic certifications are preserved where his name is Carlos Gardes. A police record of Buenos Aires province (Register 1614) also identifies as detained one Carlos Gardes, 14 years old and of French nationality. Later, his name continued appearing in 1913 as Carlos Gardes in the newspaper pieces that were mentioning the start to his famous career in the cities and villages of the province. That same year, he exchanged the final "s" of his surname for an "l", which turned out to be more resonant and pleasing to the ear.

Several authors indicate that he received an Argentinean identity card in 1914, due to the intervention of powerful political leaders. He would later lose it. But we have no evidence of what documents the artist used until 1920, when he went to the Uruguayan consulate in Buenos Aires and declared that he was born in the city of Tacuarembó. Two Uruguayan natives were on hand and bore witness to that point of origin: Juan Laguisquet and José Razzano. Gardel didn't have any birth document from that city, which prompted the need for the declaration of witnesses. José Razzano himself always considered Gardel to be native of France, although he accepted the change of birth year to 1887 introduced by Gardel from the 1890 recorded in the Toulouse register.

There were various occasions throughout Gardel's career when he had to respond evasively about his origin:

- "I was born on Corrientes Street, my country is the tango".

- "I can say my country is Argentina".

- "I'm a *porteño*, as they say in my country".

Declarations that converged into increased curiosity after his replies, and the lack of clarity that often accompanies personalities with exceptional talents who later obtain legendary characteristics. Circumstances that makes every detail of his life mysterious. It's like a double-edged sword, similar to the double axe symbolic of the ancient Cretans. On the one hand is the record relevant to how Gardel grew up, the way his inspirations came to him, what encounters with life and death tempered the genius. On the other, there is an enigmatic space unapproachable to "clear and distinct" knowledge, to the truth free from any doubts.

A few days after certifying his new details (place and date of birth, new surname) at the Uruguayan consulate in Argentina, he appeared before the Buenos Aires police on November 4, 1920 to apply for his Argentinean identity document. In March 1923, he applied for Argentinean citizenship, and obtained his passport on October 8 that year. He then traveled to Spain on November 15 with his duo partner in the *Rivera-De Rosas* theater company.

What reasons could possibly have prompted Carlos Gardel to engage in manipulating so many documents? Among the arguments that could be made, none carries greater weight than the need to elude the military obligations of his native France. In 1908, when Gardel turned 18, he was required to enlist like any other French citizen. In 1910, he would have been subject to two years of mandatory military service, an unavoidable legal regulation. In anticipation of a possible new war with Germany, that mandatory service was extended to three years by the law of August 7, 1913.

In 1914, at the start of the First World War, citizen Carlos Gardel, born in Toulouse, would have been an active reservist in the French army. However, he had lived in Buenos Aires since he was two and never contacted or registered with the French authorities. Now wishing to bring his art to international audiences, with the epicenter of notoriety being Paris, the capital of the country which won the war, Gardel needed to find an alibi that would exempt him from that serious complication.

The memory of another illustrious citizen born in France comes to mind, one who carried his obsession with unfulfilled obligations of military service with him until his death at 37. From deep in Africa, the poet Arthur Rimbaud wrote his family on February 20, 1891:

"When you answer me, tell me something about my situation regarding military service. Do I still need to do part of it?"

In Marseilles on June 24, 1981, with one leg amputated, he writes in one of his last letters to his sister:

"What is this new horror you're telling me about? What are you saying about the military service? Didn't I send you from Aden, when I was 26, a certificate that proved I was employed in a French company? That should be an exemption. And after that, every time I asked mother, she replied that everything was in order now and I had nothing to fear. Just four months ago, I asked you in one of my letters if some complaint could exist against me on this matter, because I had a desire to return to France. You never answered me, and I thought you would have already arranged everything by now. Now you lead me to believe I've been declared in default and they're pursuing me..."

By opting for Argentinean nationality and declaring himself born in Uruguay on a date different from the one recorded on his Toulouse birth certificate, Carlos Gardel was throwing any potential investigations into non-fulfillment of his military duties off the scent. That is why the formal aspects related to his documentation has given rise to a great deal of speculation, including deplorable theories that we are not going to distract ourselves with. In turn, his identification with the home country of tango is as clear as day to everyone, and Gardel added a fundamental aspect to its tradition that give it a visible profile and identity in the universal worldwide culture.

During the same period he was requesting Argentinian citizenship, Gardel enjoyed a level of recognition that exceeded that of any other popular singer, even as part of the duo. On the wings of tours in the interior of Argentina, his fame flew to different and far distant latitudes. The Teatro Nacional hired them. So did the organizers of prestigious events. The Gardel-Razzano duo was called on to sing before the Nobel Prize for Literature winner Jacinto Benavente in 1920; the Prince of Savoy in 1924, and the Prince of Wales in 1925.

Buenos Aires had in Gardel the tango singer the ideal performer and interpreter for the song that many consider the hymn of the city.

Buenos Aires, la reina del Plata,
Buenos Aires, mi tierra querida,
escuchá mi canción
que con ella va mi vida.[27]

This tango was written by Manuel Romero and put to music by Manuel Jovés in 1923. These were heady days of celebration and expansion of the tango-song, years that were crazy in their own way in Buenos Aires as well, where the bustle of large numbers of arriving immigrants was still in the process of being absorbed.

Noches porteñas, bajo tu manto
dichas y llantos muy juntos van.
Risas y besos, farra corrida,
todo se olvida con el champán.[28]

However, not everything is crowned with champagne:

Y a la salida de la milonga
se oye una nena pidiendo pan,
por eso es que en el gotan
siempre solloza una pena.[29]

The tango, child of the outskirts, now takes possession of the prosperous, ostentatious center of the city, but never forgets the other face of the city where it had its first home base. It concludes

---

[27] Buenos Aires, the queen of the Plata/ Buenos Aires, my beloved land/ Listen to my song/ for my life goes with it.

[28] Nights in the port, under your canopy/ happiness and tears go very close together/ Laughter and kisses, partying around/ you forget everything with champagne.

[29] And coming out from the milonga hall/ You hear a little girl begging for bread/ That's the reason why in the "gotán"/ you always hear a sob of pain and sorrow

(Note: Gotán is a variant spelling of tango, created for rhyme and poetic reasons)

with verses that Gardel surely sang with every bit of the heartfelt emotion contained in the lyrics:

Buenos Aires, cual a una querida,
si estás lejos mejor hay que amarte.
Y decir toda la vida:
antes morir que olvidarte. [30]

In 1923, he recorded this tango with the acoustic system, accompanied by Barbieri and Ricardo on guitars. He went back to record it in 1930 in two different versions, one with guitars that was never released, and the other featuring piano, violin and guitars.

Lyrics and music

The decade that the tango enjoyed its popular breakthrough, the 1920s, was one of extraordinary changes in the *rioplantense* popular arts. The *criollo* theater world chose, almost invariably, to include the performance of tangos on stage. It often served as the synthesis of the theatrical play and frequently featured the lyrics and music played by the orchestras live and later recorded on discs. From that master channel of creations inspired by city life, the tango would develop renowned talents as lyricists, writers skilled at handling the theatrical action that reduced the piece to that dramatic essence that makes a good sung tango.

The technical revolution was underway in the music scene. It was undertaken by young musicians who wrote down on staff paper the notes to the new compositions and the arrangements for performance. The tango was played with the score in front of the

---

[30] Buenos Aires, as with any woman you loved/ the farther away you are, the better to love you/ And to be able to say your entire life/ I'd rather die first before I forget you.

musician. The impact was so powerful that neither conventions nor condemnations could stand up to it. The middle-class youth who prospered in affluent Argentina were studying theory and instrumentation in order to play it. The most elegant locales for entertainment were injected with fresh life by tango orchestras whose basic line-up consisted of the *Sexteto Típico*. Carlos Gardel lived the night life with the composers and performers of the new tango. Whether it was his personal nature or simply destiny, he was always at the forefront of the music. During that era, he connected with De Caro, Arolas, Firpo, and Fresedo. In 1934, at the height of his fame, he performed at a private party in New York accompanied by the *bandoneón* of 13-year-old Astor Piazzolla.

The girlfriend

In 1920 Gardel met a young girl named Isabel Martínez del Valle who would enjoy the status of being the singer's acknowledged girlfriend for years. She was 14 years old and Gardel was 29. It was his longest-lasting relationship and documented through the letters Gardel sent to Isabel. They never made their relationship public, due to a certain stubborn discretion he observed throughout his life that also fell in line with the wishes of the show business companies, who preferred their leading men to be "eternal bachelors". She received and sent numerous letters to him that helped ease the absences of her boyfriend. Once she traveled to Europe with him and closer to home in Argentina and Uruguay on other occasions. They were frequently seen together at theaters and cabarets, as well as the usual private parties with friends. They lived together in the same house for periods of time, the "love nest", residences rented by Gardel, according to the letters. One was in Rodríguez Peña Street and another on the corner of Corrientes and Callao. Later he bought a house in Directorio Street. From what we know, Isabel generally adapted to the conditions that the work and professionalism of an artist

Isabel Martínez del Valle:
Carlos Gardel's longtime girlfriend.

involved. At one time, she attempted to start an opera career, and even traveled to Milan in 1931 to study with soprano Giannina Ruzz, but without any notable benefit for her professional aspirations. There is evidence they traveled together in Italy that year. However, the relationship lived it most splendid moments in Buenos Aires. In one of Gardel's agendas, for June 28, 1929, you can read: "Don't forget. Biógrafo [movie] and Chantecler [cabaret] with Isabel". The letters they exchanged confess their mutual affection for each other. They surely had their good times and bad times, periods of passion and disenchantment. This relationship would probably occupy the calm place in Gardel's love life, as they would maintain it without the girlfriend proposing they make it official...or her relatives demanding money.

The relationship involved many scenes of playfulness, pranks and mischief, as Isabel herself remarked: "Gardel was like a big kid". Her memory kept the life of the artist in safe hands, recalling two undeniable traits: his preoccupation with studying the content of the lyrics he was singing ("You don't have to sing like a parrot," Gardel told her) and the mediocre songs he sometimes recorded to help out friends who were down on their luck. Concerning his infidelities, Isabel declared: "The one he loved was me, so it didn't matter very much to me..." In any case, Carlos Gardel never flaunted his love affairs, protecting himself at all times with a strong sense of discretion.

After the accident in Medellín, Isabel's role grew larger in the vacuum left behind by Carlos Gardel's death. She was the subject of photographs and interviews where she declared they had plans to marry. However, as we will see below, the last letter by Gardel to his agent states the opposite.

The subject of Gardel's love life provided a good deal of ink in the gossip magazines. Behind the veil of discretion carefully set up by Gardel himself and watched over by his loyal friends, there are more than enough accounts of intense, albeit brief, love affairs along the different paths he traveled during his extraordinary

career. Always accompanying his gentlemanly avoidance of
rumors and gossip was an unwavering interest in his professional
well-being and presenting his art.

3. FIRST TRIPS TO SPAIN (1923-1927)

Relations between Spain and its former colonies were going through a period of reconciliation. Peru and Ecuador selected Spain as the arbitrator to define and settle their border disputes, resulting in the final "not subject to appeal" ruling in 1904.

The war in Cuba (1898, the Spanish-American War) was already part of history. In one way or another, that conflict warned of the growing pressure of North American imperialism at the expense of the Latin American community. The Spanish generation of '98[31], after considering Spain's internal domestic situation and international reputation in the world, encouraged an overt opening up towards the various Latin American nations. Relations grew closer and deeper and, of course, Spanish-speaking America was a natural destination for the heavy emigration of Spaniards forced to move away from their native land due to food shortages and lack of work. Those factors were only aggravated by the extraordinary demographic explosion that

---

[31] The Spanish generation of 1898: A group of young Spanish writers, essayists, and poets who were profoundly affected by the moral, political and social crisis triggered in Spain by the military defeat suffered in the Spanish-American War in 1898 and resulting loss of the colonies of Puerto Rico, Guam, Cuba and the Philippines.

Photograph taken during the first Gardel-Razzano trip to Spain
with the Rivera-De Rosas theatre group (1923).
Razzano is standing at the far left and Gardel at the far right.

occurred at the end of the 19th century. Some emigrants to the
Americas came back telling fabricated tales of great success. The
shipping companies immediately went to work promoting the
dream of easy commercial opportunities awaiting people to
encourage traveling there. José Ortega Munilla wrote of that
immigration: "It is a dream, a delirium, a fever that no medicine
can cure". The figures alone should serve for an example:
1,036,662 Spaniards emigrated to Argentina between 1900 and
1915.

The continual coming and going of theatrical and musical
shows between Spain and the Americas was part of that flow, once
you recognize the common bonds linking these audiences
connected by the Atlantic Ocean, a body of water which had
changed from being *mare ignotus* (unknown sea) to *mare nostrum*
(our sea).

In 1923, the *Rivera-De Rosa* company embarked from Buenos

Aires for an artistic tour of Spain. As a unique and no doubt colorful element, the cast included the Gardel-Razzano duo with their guitarists José Ricardo and Guillermo Barbieri. The voyage was documented by direct witness accounts. Spanish journalist Serrano Claver, a fellow traveler on the German transatlantic steamer *Antonio Delfino*, would write: "The peace on the boat is upset by the uproar from the showbiz crowd as they shout, applaud, sing and laugh". Apparently, the party wasn't limited to the theater company and their friends from Buenos Aires but extended to other passengers aboard the ship. A letter sent to Carlos Gardel from Sao Paulo, Brazil on November 24, 1933, recalls that trip. A very beautiful and concise piece of literature that eloquently makes clear:

"Carlos:
It is never too late when one remembers... *Antonio Delfino*, a delightful trip. 1923, Paris Hotel; Sarmiento and Florida, 1925... Your little Brazilian, Ñatita... Do you still remember me? I don't believe you... I've never forgotten.
My congratulations on your hit *Espérame*. It would be very kind of you to answer me right away. I continue being your admirer, Elsita
P.S. You can write to:
Rue Salvador Lerma, 14. Sao Paulo, Brasil, Senhorita Elsa Braga".

The steamship docked at the port of Vigo. The company continued its journey from there, traveling to Madrid where it performed at the Teatro Apolo. Members of the royal family of King Alfonso XIII attended the performance, including Queen Victoria Eugenia and the famous princess Isabella, *La Chata*. Writers like Jacinto Benavente, bullfighters like Ignacio Sánchez Mejía, and a long list of illustrious personalities of that era joined them. After the festive finale, a gaucho segment featuring the Gardel-Razzano duo, the company moved on to the Teatro Price. Still resplendent in the spectacular attire typical of gauchos from the Pampas, Carlos Gardel sang some of the tangos in his repertoire by himself. The Madrid press praised their skills as singers and guitarists this way:

> "The theater was full and you can rest assured it will be full every night these artists are performing".

There would be nights out on the town full of good times and colorful incidents, but also a recognized professionalism on the part of the artists when it was time to perform.

The duo left for France in the middle of January 1924. The first stop was Toulouse, where Gardel met up with his mother, who was visiting her family at the time. They had ended up accepting Berta's decisions and the paths those choices had led her down without any misgivings.

From Toulouse, the duo traveled to Paris to see some tourist sites and do some shopping. After finishing off all the money earned from their recent gigs (like so many times before), they made the voyage back to Buenos Aires, where recording and performing commitments were awaiting them. In fact, they only recorded three songs together that year. The rest of the 78 songs recorded during 1924 were sung by Gardel solo, with most of the pieces being tangos.

The wear and tear was beginning to take its toll on Razzano's voice. At the same time, he was gradually assuming the role of Gardel's manager for arranging his performances, handling the incoming money and supervising expenses, searching for material to add to the repertoire, contracts, etc. The Variety Artists Association gradually grew in importance, and Pepe Razzano would further increase his strong ties with the organization. The duo toured the provinces in Argentina and performed on a powerful new communications media that established itself during that era, the radio.

Tango, city, salon

The city is the most archetypal element of the tango, as we said before. The urban maze was the site where the tango artists found the tempting, inviting spaces enabling them to expand on and develop their talents. The tango calls the hole-in-the-wall joints and dives home, aspires to the concert halls and the conquest of Paris, proudly flaunting its mixed character, the *orillero* outsider, happy-go-lucky and serious, libertine and formal. The tango has

Gardel in Spain

made its way in the world ever since, winning people over, conquering it. It wasn't created to persuade the masses looking to follow leaders. It is the subtle distinction, perhaps a marvelous one, of the modern city dweller. It lives from the confidence that comes from sharing personal intimacy, before giving your allegiance to a flag or the whims of a leader. That accounts for its democratic nature, an egalitarian flowering that takes place in halls on the outskirts or the center. It always tends to level off and eliminate any hierarchies in favor of the person best suited for the dance on the dance floor.

The subject matter of the lyrics expresses those values. You can also say it hints at self-criticism of the perspectives it holds almost sacred. There are tango lyrics that appear to be written based on another tango, presenting values contrary to those in the original song. The reason may lie in the fact that everything can fit in its lyrics: the words found in another tango sung by Gardel, *¿Por Qué Soy Reo?*, directly opposes the content of the archetypal tango *Mi Noche Triste*:

> *En mi bulín mistongo*
> *no hay cintas, ni moñitos,*
> *ni aquellos retratitos*
> *que cita la canción...*[32]

Together with the variety of characters, the persistence of the dramatic action is also present as a characteristic trait of tango lyrics. The scenes described are always in motion, constantly animated by a desire for a story that always includes some movement of life.

After clarifying these points, we insist that in the decade of the

---

[32] In my miserable apartment/ there are no ribbons, no bows/ none of the little pictures/ the song mentions...

'20s, except for some writers, politicians and rich kids of the repressed aristocracy who rejected it, tango lovers reveled in the physical invitation to dance the tango. That is why they felt they were represented in Gardel's song. For his backing arrangements, *El Morocho* wisely moved away from the orchestras except on a handful of select occasions. Only guitars that left the singer and his voice naked in front of the audience. And there went Gardel, bringing the words written by others to the forefront through his singing, delivering them at just the right tempo, making the content of the lyrics inseparable from the music surrounding them. He frequently introduced changes in the texts himself to improve the spoken message, the person-to-person quality. There are time-consuming projects underway that propose to compare the original lyrics with those actually sung by Gardel, to point out the changes introduced during the performance. Even more astonishing, he incorporated changes into the songs that varied from take to take. In some cases, five or six takes were needed before he found the best way to express the lyrics for the recorded master.

Horses, tangos, travels

Racehorses represented an area of special interest in Gardel's life. Not to mention the other horses, the "comrades" we should say, because in the prosperous farming and ranching country that was Argentina in that period, the "equestrian status" occupied a privileged place in the collective imagination. For the gaucho, to walk or be on foot was one of the worst disgraces imaginable. When they asked one of the last gaucho leaders, Chacho Peñaloza, how he was doing in exile, he replied:

- "What do you think? I'm in Chile and on foot".

The poetry of the folk singers' oral and written tradition gives a good account of a culture that developed on horseback, both in the mountains and the plains. The first and best-known songs sung by Gardel included titles celebrating special horses, notably *El Moro* and *El Pangaré*, both recorded in 1917. Stories about men on horseback were honored in the collective imagination of Argentina so it was only natural that Gardel would be involved in gaucho circles right from his very earliest days. However, the urban

Gardel and one of his best friends:
Jockey Irineo Leguisamo.

configuration that marked the development of the country as a modern nation left its mark on it. The country rituals became urbanized at the racetracks, as middle and upper-class Argentinians turned out for the spectacle and thrills of the races and betting action. We'll look back at the episode of November 16, 1918 as an example from the numerous ones documented in anecdotes, memoirs, letters and books. The Gardel-Razzano duo was appearing in the town of General Pico (La Pampa province), performing along with the tango orchestra of Roberto Firpo, who was responsible for the entire cast of artists. In addition to singing, Gardel and Razzano were joking around and on the lookout for good times. Among the hijinks that poor Firpo had to suffer through was the pair running off during the night. After a long train ride, they made it for the end of a race featuring two famous horses, Botafogo and Grey Fox. The next day Firpo was forced to apologize for the duo's absence to the audience and promoter while his companions on the tour enjoyed a good, long laugh at his expense.

Time passed by and visits to the racetrack were constant. "Every Sunday", as one tango goes. By 1925, Gardel was in good enough financial shape to have his own racehorse, *Lunático*, even though he didn't have a stable to keep him. But as fate would have it, his lifelong friend Francisco Maschio owned one. *Lunático* was a thoroughbred with good bloodlines, but his performance was mediocre despite all the loving care and fame of its owner. Once his racing life at the track was over, they put him out to stud on a ranch in Santa Fe. He was a stud stallion there until 1933 when, at the express wish of his owner, he was taken to open pastures to live out the rest of his days in freedom. Carlos Gardel bought a total of six more racehorses afterwards. Their fortunes varied and his enthusiasm had its up-and-down spells. Gardel placed bets via telegrams sent to his agent in Buenos Aires, without cutting back on his concert appearances, for the racetracks in Montevideo, Paris and New York.

During that golden age of racetracks in Argentina, the most

August 1925: Gardel-Razzano and their two guitarists en route to Huetel to sing for the Prince of Wales. It turned out to be one of the last times they officially sang together.

famous jockey was Ireneo Leguisamo, nicknamed *El Mono* (The Monkey), one of Gardel's closest friends. When he was in Nice once, Gardel invited *El Mono* to come down on a trip to the French Riviera *(Cote d'Azur)*, home to the most elegant beaches, hotels and fashion salons in Europe. There are any number of tangos with lyrics about horses and races; perhaps the best, and best-known, is *Leguisamo Solo*, which Gardel sang and recorded in Barcelona in 1926 and then again in Buenos Aires in 1927. In the jockey's memoir compiled by Daniel Alfonso Luro, *Leguisamo de Punta a Punta*, there are revealing references to his friendship with Carlos Gardel, whose interest in the turf world never waned despite the ever-increasing demands of his artistic activity that required him to spend months and years outside Argentina. In a letter to his agent from New York in 1934, he says:

> "Dear Armando, morning bank draft. Bet 500 slips by halves; arrange expenses, win or lose, telegraph right away content. Say hello to Francisco and Mono for me. Affectionately. Be strong".

In the same vein, and most likely when he was suffering from losing money and disappointing performances, Gardel says to Defino again in a later letter from Bogota on June 20, 1935:

> "When I reach New York, I'll send you the full amount. You take that little bit of money earned by working my butt off doing everything I could and save it. As for the horses, it's good that you're looking around for buyers to sell them off. I'm fed up with losing money in the world of horses."

End of the Gardel-Razzano Duo (1925)

During the 1920s, the British Empire was the leading buyer of Argentinean exports and consequently enjoyed special treatment. In 1925, Argentina received a visit from the Prince of Wales, who would become King Edward VIII and, after his abdication, the Duke of Windsor. His intention was to familiarize himself and tighten relations with countries in the area of English influence. The Argentinean government received him with pomp and circumstance at the estate of the landowner Unzué de Casares. The Gardel-Razzano duo was invited to join the ministers and military officers, and apparently it was their performance that most excited the Prince. The echoes from that performance occupied a great deal of space in the press reports that praised the importance of the *criollo* song form and the tango at the reception party, and the favorable disposition of the future monarch towards those *rioplantense* sounds.

Nevertheless, the countdown leading to the end of the duo had started. A month after those happy weeks, Razzano felt his ability to sing was seriously compromised and proposed to retire for a period of time. Gardel encouraged him to undergo treatment with León Elkin, a doctor who had treated him on another occasion, and simultaneously appointed him as manager of his business affairs, as previously noted. He had already been coping with the weight of solo live performances and recording sessions for a fair amount of time. In November 1925, he embarked on his second tour of Spain with guitarist José Ricardo, once again integrated into the show of the *Rivera-De Rosas* company. On this trip, the singer was being heavily advertised as an individual artist, forging his own path independently of the between acts appearances and end-of-theater-run parties. In December, he recorded 21 tunes in Barcelona and was hired to perform in Madrid during the difficult month of January, when money was often scarce after all the holiday spending. But there was a full house at the Teatro Romea every day, and the scheduled 10-day engagement wound up

Gardel in the house he bought for his mother
and himself in 1927.

turning into 30 days of performances. It was his voice with the
most minimal accompaniment of his great career, one guitar, that
warranted the rapturous audience response. In February, he went
back to Barcelona for more recording.

He returned to Buenos Aires on March 23, 1926, to perform, record and expand his repertoire with new material. We are keeping in mind that the birthplace of the tango was there, the social, historical and aesthetic environment where its extraordinary world was created. Although there were significant competitors among the singers there, Argentina acknowledged Gardel's status in a certain sense with several meaningful gestures. He was the first to record there with the electrical system he had already tested out in Barcelona. He would also perform the winning tangos at the 1926 Gran Fiesta del Tango at the Cine Grand Splendid in Buenos Aires. A competition selected six songs to receive their public debut that night. The orchestra of Osvaldo Fresedo performed the chosen pieces. Gardel sang three of the songs to such great popular acclaim that he had to repeat the performances. He later recorded five of the six titles.

Benefit concerts and spontaneous performances

Since this was a period in which the associations for protecting the copyrights of songwriters and performers were still very precarious, the artists developed wide-ranging means of supporting each other. They called them "benefit concerts" and they generally consisted of a succession of different artists taking to the stage to offer a sample of their art. Artists who had health problems, or were suffering economic and social difficulties, received this assistance from their colleagues. There were also benefit performances for the "Doormen and Ushers of the Teatro Empire", the new Variety Artists Association, and the Newspaper Vendors Nursing Home.

These are plenty of these performances listed in the artistic timeline of both the Gardel-Razzano duo and Gardel advertised as a solo artist. Actors, leaders of dance companies, singers, writers, *payadores*, etc., were all beneficiaries of those concerts over the years.

In turn, Gardel's inclination to sing at informal reunions with his friends are another significant feature of his career. The Café de los Angelitos was one traditional spot for the artistic crowd to get together. Gardel knew it was important to appear in public sometimes against the wishes of his partner Razzano, who argued that he should take care of his voice. Another habitual place for these spontaneous events was Francisco Maschio's stable, where Gardel's racehorses were kept and cared for.

In those environments the singer's fondness for comic tales and witty jokes were well known. He was capable of gathering enough people around him to keep a continuing thread going from one joke to the next, achieving some truly uproarious sessions among the boys out to have a good time.

The poet Rafael Alberti tells one interesting anecdote. After attending a football game in Santander, Spain in May, 1928 (a game won by Barcelona), he writes:

"That night, we joined the Catalonians at the hotel. The Catalonia anthem 'Els Segadors' was sung, and one person who had been with us during the game masterfully sang Argentinean tangos that were truly beautiful. It was Carlos Gardel.

We left in the early morning hours for Palencia. Gardel was a healthy, unpretentious, emotional guy. He celebrated everything that he saw and heard. Our trip through the city was noisy and boisterous. The names of the store owners fascinated us. Crude, primitive, names taken from Roman and Visigothic martyrs. We were reading them in delight and couldn't stop ourselves from cracking up: "Pasamanería of Hubilibrordo González", "Café of Genciano Gómez", "Almacén of Eutimio Bustamante", and especially this one: "Repuestos of Cojoncio Pérez". It was a happy, fast, unforgettable trip. Months later, when I was in Madrid, I received a card from Gardel postmarked from Buenos Aires. He sent me his best wishes, along with a big hug, for Cojoncio Pérez[33]. Just like me, that was what most impressed him in Palencia".

---

[33] The joke: the name Cojoncio is close to "cojones", one Spanish word for testicles or balls. Loosely translated, Gardel is sending his regards to "Big Balls" Pérez.

Tango singer in his prime (1925-1931)

The tangos now formed the musical center of gravity for Carlos Gardel. His artistic life was analyzed just a little less than his daily life, He was interviewed in Buenos Aires and recalled his second trip to Spain at great length and with considerable affection. Since that tour, Spain embraced him as the most important figure of the tango. In turn, the tango was viewed there as a tradition in its own right, an original style of Argentinean music:

> "You can judge how big it was by one fact: the tour and my contract was to sing for 10 days and I had to stay there for two months... The audience took to me with what you can call genuine affection," Gardel explained.

Later he said:

> "In my circle of friends, I hung around with Miguel Fleta, the great opera tenor. We struck up a sincere friendship... and incidentally, I found Santiago Rusiñol, the great writer and painter, over there. Whenever we got together, Rusiñol always remembered our country and asked me about people of letters and journalists who were his friends. And sang tangos".

In *El Alma que Canta* magazine dated April 6, 1926, he added:

> "In conclusion, the tango is as popular in Spain today as it is in Buenos Aires. Truthfully, the tango has done more to increase the bond and brotherhood between our two nations as all the efforts by diplomats put together".

We really find ourselves now in the years that the most fervent fans of Gardel's work consider his best. A five-year journey running from 1926 to 1931, the era when Gardel begins to become established as a film star. It is the period when he makes the greatest number of recordings and was fully empathizing with the stories he was singing. There are singular poets, inevitable names to recall: Enrique Cadícamo, known today worldwide for *Nostalgia* and *Los Mareados*; Francisco García Jiménez, *Siga el Corso*; Esteban Celedonio Flores *Mano a Mano*; Enrique Santos Discépolo, *Yira-Yira, Cambalache*. However, the number of songwriters not included in that list is so significant that you can speak of this era as a genuine golden age of songwriters. And every one of them was interested in having Gardel include their pieces in his repertoire. In effect, he did just that. We feel it is worth pointing out again the prodigious effort involved in the daily work of rehearsing, performing and recording that was required of the singer. Several authors have said that Gardel made "a genuine creation" out of their songs, leaving the form he recorded them in incapable of being improved on. It is certainly his finest, most glorious moment as a performer. He did not compose during this period and dedicated all his genius to interpretation and performance. If we keep in mind the figure of close to 900 different songs recorded, the general reference made of his music is that the recordings only represent 20% of his complete body of work. Apart from the constant release of recordings available on the market at all times, fresh anthologies appear every now and then that may result in a new "revelation" about Gardel. To enjoy him and know him is to listen repeatedly to *Volver, Milonga Sentimental, Mi Buenos Aires Querido, Mano a Mano, La Cumparsita…* But that is only beginning to scratch the surface of the enormous talent on display in such an extensive and original discography.

It was clear that Carlos Gardel was so caught up in the radical nature of being a tango singer and he will deliver the best of himself, what he has left behind for us. The tango exists as a finished creation, something acknowledged by musicians, poets, and singers alike, based on the definitive form that Gardel gave it. He gained the status of an international star on his second tour of Spain and his rise to stardom was permanent, as indicated by the prolific number of recording sessions starting from this period. In the same vein, it must be added that the discs authorized to be pressed for release on the market were not all the recordings he made. A good number of them were rejected as substandard, although time has judged the opposite from what he decided of the performances. New discoveries and/or releases of test pressings periodically appear that were not released commercially during the artist's lifetime. They are generally versions discarded for technically defective recording, mistakes made in singing the words, bad sound quality, etc. Nevertheless, they are posthumously released several decades after being recorded and Gardel's death, and his followers buy them with genuine interest. In other cases, they are sold to people who don't even notice the origin of the product but simply wish to listen to the singer, nothing more. The pieces that were possible for us to track and verify to date are included in the discography at the end of this book. You can be sure other discs will be added to future lists, since the increase in the number of releases will be incessant.

The first recordings by Carlos Gardel using the electrical system (replacing the impression of sound based on mechanical [acoustic] impulses by electrical ones, in addition to incorporating a microphone instead of the receptor horn) took place in Barcelona on December 26, 1925. A total of 63 magnificent pieces were produced in the city with the electrical system during his stay there. He made the initial recordings there accompanied only by the guitar of José Ricardo. The next ones were recorded using more instruments, including violin and piano with the guitars in some cases.

On his return to Buenos Aires, he also recorded his voice using the electrical system, accompanied by Ricardo and Barbieri. But, ever vigilant and conscientious about the final result of the takes, he discarded them and went back to record the songs again using the acoustic system. He tried the electrical system again in Buenos Aires on December 30, 1926 and found the results far superior. From that point on, he will only record using that method and would do so later in Paris and New York.

In the book *Historia Artística de Carlos Gardel*, by Miguel Ángel Morena, there is a documented tracking of the singer's life. At the time of publication, there are hundreds of texts published with landmarks that highlight different aspects of his career, from the mundane details of his everyday life to the extraordinary. The lengthy journey, as detailed, began to gain significance following his youthful adventures in the neighborhood bordering the Mercado de Abasto in Buenos Aires. Then came the meeting with José Razzano, Martino and Saúl Salinas, to tour around the bars and theaters of the capital city and provinces. After that, the acclaim given the national duo in 1914 up to the advent of the tango-song initiated by Gardel in 1917. If we jump ahead to July 24, 1926, we find him performing in the Teatro Smart as a solo artist accompanied by his guitarists Ricardo and Barbieri in a festival honoring the crew members of the hydroplane *Buenos Aires*. Other actors and singers were also featured on stage at that event. The tango was represented onstage by the orchestra of Francisco Canaro in addition to Gardel. Casimiro Aín, the *Vasquito* (Little Basque), and his partner María Scotto danced with Canaro's orchestra behind them. The couple had performed an exhibition on January 1, 1924, before Pope Pius XI (so that the pope would lift the ecclesiastical condemnation that weighed heavily on the tango dance). Apart from that occasion we want to point to another no less frequent one: Carlos Gardel shared the stage with jazz big bands and opera singers. At the Florida movie theater in September that year, Gardel was part of the program together with Francisco Lomuto's orchestra and the González Jazz Band. A pattern for a live show that anticipated the stellar days he experienced years later in Parisian theaters.

Concert poster from the 1927-28 tour of Spain.

Third trip to Spain (1927-1928)

Contrary to what the popular refrain says, Gardel had no need to show that the third time's the charm. He had triumphed on his two previous tours and this current one would confirm his rise to stardom on Spanish soil. But to where? He felt excited on reaching the port in Barcelona, exultant over returning to the country he and his fellow Argentineans called "the motherland". He brought a significant new repertoire with him to add to the songs that were already audience favorites when Gardel sang them on the previous tour. In his bags, he carried two tangos by Spanish songwriters he planned to debut: *La Cieguita* and *Mi Dolor*. Shortly after disembarking, he appeared on a program on Catalonian radio, announcing his performance with Ricardo and Barbieri in the Principal Palace. He appeared there from November 11 to December 4, 1927. After his performances, he never missed the late-night sessions, whether they were dinners with friends or "strolls to burn calories". He traveled to Madrid to perform at the Teatro Romea, where he had overcome the *cuesta de enero* (difficult January) the year before, as both the aristocracy and the humble everyday people applauded him with equal intensity. He became good friends with Spanish artists, along with well-known Argentineans in Spain like the Canaro brothers. Rafael had an orchestra performing in Madrid and the older brother, Francisco, enjoyed a successful recording career him. He also created a group that was popular in Spain for many years, the Irusta-Fugazot-Demare trio who were the second major star during the golden years of tango on the Iberian peninsula.

The Spanish journalist José Montero Alonso wrote in a report about Gardel:

"Among the good girls of Madrid, afternoons at the Royalty, teas at the Ritz, Sundays along the Castellana, steering wheel, close-cropped hair, the Charleston, Gardel can count on frivolous romantic devotions. They listen to his songs over and over again, and applaud him, imitating his moving accent. In the well-mannered shrine of these girls, the name, the figure and the art of Carlos Gardel has claimed a very prominent spot now. The tango (have you seen Gardel's admirable style of singing that *Cieguita?*) has passed before us once again with its old and much-loved emotional breezes".

José Moreno Alonso inserted the following reply from Gardel to those extensive remarks:

"If I would be born ten times over, and you would ask me in any one of them what I wanted to be or do in life, I would only answer with a single word: to sing, to sing... My attraction to the stage? Always. I've had it since I was a little kid this big. My dream was to be up on the same stages that the great singers performed on when they came through Buenos Aires".

During these same dates in Spain, he lent his image to a colorful advertisement that publicized a hair gel, Gomina Argentine. Gardel wrote on it himself, underneath the sales order information for the product next to his well-groomed image:

"The Argentine hair gel is as indispensable to me as the guitar. Carlos Gardel".

He said goodbye to the year 1927 in the now-defunct Mesón del Sevillano restaurant in the company of the Canaro brothers and the Irusta-Fugazot-Demare Trio. It was a tango and criolla farewell to the year in the capital of Spain.

He had to return to Barcelona to record more discs on January 9, 1928 and once again fulfill his commitments at the theater. What did he record? Among the 30 songs recorded to disc were memorable takes of noteworthy landmarks in his career, like *Mano a Mano, La Cieguita, La Cumparsita, Siga el Corso, Tabernero, Traicionera, Pato, La Borrachera del Tango*. José

1929: Contract committing Gardel to ten days of shows in Madrid. Gardel visited Barcelona and Madrid after his tremendous success in France. It would be the last time he officially performed in Spain.

Ricardo and Guillermo Barbieri accompanied him.

Montserrat Guillemat and Nieto del Molino had composed a tango they titled *La Gloria del Águila*, a reference to the great feat of Ramón Franco who, together with Ruiz with de Alda Durán y Rada, joined Madrid and Buenos Aires together with the flight of the hydroplane *Plus Ultra*. Gardel debuted it at the theater in Barcelona without announcing it beforehand in the program. The impact on the audience was tremendous and their applause forced them to repeat it several times. The *El Imparcial* daily newspaper in Madrid, commented in January 1928:

> "He deliberately excludes from the programs the compositions that are well known and being popular, are ones that we would like to hear. Everything he sings is new, his own, you could say, and his performance was surprising in every way at the Romea. The theater was completely sold out and the distinguished Buenos Aires artist was forced to repeat performances countless times in response to the persistent cheers and applause. Mr. Gardel was accompanied by two guitarists who were also quite accomplished".

The performances in Barcelona were followed by appearances in Bilbao, San Sebastian and Santander. And then he went back to Barcelona again for another round of appearances. In his comings and goings to the Catalonian capital, Gardel struck up a close friendship with the players of the city's star football club.

It seems appropriate to re-emphasize some details that are resonating in our memory regarding the time Gardel spent in Spain during these periods. We already indicated this country formed his first base of support and projection, the springboard that catapulted him to an international career. After long, well-received tours, he would be ready for his future stellar performances. The artist matures, becomes familiar with the demands and flatteries that go along with fame, learning the ropes for representing an expression of *rioplatense* culture that became universal, and formed an irreplaceable cog of that cultural expression. He appears in the press, the salons, football stadiums, the festivals and streets of Spanish cities. The theaters where his performances took place were attended by common people and the refined nobility, artists, sports personalities, producers... Gardel defines his persona there as being open to all society while taking maximum advantage of the technical resources available to him. He cuts dozens of discs in Barcelona, like his first, superior recordings using the electrical method. He repeatedly refers to Spain with genuine emotion as the mother country. And who does he single out so memorably in his last public relations message, saying that he dedicates these recently finished, better performances to "his friends in Spain and Latin America".

His stays in the city also coincided with the presence of the players from the Argentinean national team, who arrived in town to play the Barcelona team before going on to the Olympic Games in Amsterdam. He honored the Argentinean players, cheered them on in their victories and consoled them in defeat. He guided them around Barcelona and Paris, so they could become familiar with the streets and go shopping. The dinner Gardel treated them to in a Montmarte restaurant became famous and was topped off with champagne at the Cabaret Palermo. This evening was recorded for posterity by the most important Argentinean sports magazine, *El Gráfico*, which opened up its pages to include a photograph of the singer, highlight his place in the tango world and a sizable news item referring to the party:

> "He has earned the honor of this news item because, first in Barcelona and later in Paris, he was together with the Argentinean players encouraging them all the time. He has earned that honor because he is the one fellow countryman who soothed the souls of our boys with his guitar in foreign lands. They went to Spain and France and he followed them. He arrived in Paris with them. And in honor of them, he gave a dinner with champagne that was attended by however many poor Argentineans there may be in Paris. Montmarte had a real criolla night that night".

Gardel was in Paris due to his desire to present himself to the city that was the capital of the arts and entertainment. And perhaps also still a fundamental center of international political wheeling and dealing.

4. PREPARATIONS TO PERFORM IN PARIS (1928)

The stay in Paris accompanying the Argentinean Olympic team was not the only thing that kept Gardel busy in April and May of 1928. On May 18, he signed a contract to perform in Paris, Nice, and Biarritz, but he had to return to Buenos Aires first to honor commitments for recording discs and performances contracted by his manager José Razzano.

His arrival on the famous trans-Atlantic liner Conte Rosso (mentioned in the tango *Barajando*) was reported in the press and attracted much attention in the Argentinean arts scene. Not to mention the stir caused in the Buenos Aires streets by his Graham-Paige luxury car, a gift from the Catalonians.

> "Tell me if that's not another beautiful memory of them to hang on to!" he declared.

He performed in Buenos Aires and Montevideo. On July 9, the anniversary of Argentina's declaration of independence, radio station Radio Prieto prepared an extensive program that included opera singers, tango and jazz artists before an invited live audience. In the days following that concert, Gardel's two guitarists incorporated José María Aguilar, famed for his picking technique and what was known as the "mandolin effect", into the ensemble. However, his addition ultimately angered José Ricardo, the guitarist with the longest tenure in the group, so much that he stopped accompanying Gardel the following year, 1929, after 12 years and over 600 songs recorded with the singer.

The preparations for his future performance in Paris were meticulous and painstaking. With the three guitarists, Gardel prepared an extensive, wide-ranging repertoire that encompassed his entire career arc. This period found Gardel shining on songs that were humorous, warnings, tongue-in-cheek and inspirational. It was a time when the tango palette displaying its extraordinary variety, one that proved any of the old generalizations that limited it to themes of loss and betrayal in love were outdated and untrue. Gardel included pieces by Cadícamo and Discépolo, who were at the height of their creative powers in writing tangos. He sang some classic tangos from his repertoire, but he was always open to expanding the range of material he performed. On the other hand, in Buenos Aires, Montevideo, and even Spain, a plethora of tangos were being composed and singers were emerging to perform them on the cabaret stage, radio, and in cafes and taverns. How can you not recall *Victoria, Traicionera, Pato, Che Papusa, oí, Malevaje, Haragán, Mano Cruel, Che Bartolo* from those times?

Let's take a look at some of them. Discépolo produced a revolution in the lyrical conception when he wrote *Malevaje* (Outlaws). For the music, he chose a highly individual composer, Juan de Dios Filiberto, who didn't agree much with the title, since he thought the tango should "dignify itself". However, the song still wound up asking at the beginning and end, just like *Malevaje*:

Decí por Dios que me has dao
que estoy tan cambiao
no sé más quien soy. [34]

---

[34] I said, my God, what you have done to me? / I'm changed so much/ that I don't know who I am any more.

Meanwhile, the main character explains his radical transformation from love. His peers, who have stayed true to their old habits, don't know what's come over him:

El malevaje extrañao
me mira sin comprender,
me ve perdiendo el cartel
de guapo que ayer
brillaba en la acción.
No ve que estoy embretao
vencido y maniao
en tu corazón. [35]

"When there is a confession, you need no proof," says the legal formula. For the individual who reduces his being-in-the-world to the dagger in his hand, ready to flash it in a second in the duel, the experience of being hurt by love that happened to him will change his values. He repeats the explanation for that change, but it is also sudden and unstoppable:

Te vi pasar tangueando altanera
con un compás tan hondo y sensual
que no fue más que verte y perder
la fe, el coraje y el ansia e 'guapear [36]

Other texts have noted that the importance the tango establishes in the sequence of the dancers is significant, as if they would rise up to their highest possibilities of seduction. *No fue más*

---

[35] The local outlaws are surprised/ they look at me without understanding/ They see me losing the reputation/ as the brave guy who yesterday/ was shining in the action/ They don't see that I'm corralled/ beaten and hung out to season/ in your heart.

[36] I saw you pass by dancing the tango so full of pride/ with a rhythm so deep and sensual/ That all it took was to see you and I lose/ Faith, courage, and longing to play the brave guy.

que verte y perder / la fe, el coraje y el ansia e'guapear (All it took was to see you and I lose/ faith, courage, and longing to play the brave guy). *Guapear* is used here in the sense that the meaning often has in *rioplatense* Spanish. In this case, *guapo* is the brave guy, in other contexts it often means the one who does the best work. The man in love now doesn't dare to *guapear*, to risk his life by fighting, because:

> *Ayer, de miedo a matar,*
> *en vez de pelear*
> *me puse a correr...* [37]

A fact that is extremely strange and disgraceful. The iconography of the characters from the period had no place for anyone who ran away from a fight. However, in this salutary lesson of Discépolo's creation, the subject adds:

> *Me vi a la sombra o finao*
> *pensé en no verte y temblé...*
> *Si yo que nunca aflojé*
> *de noche angustiao*
> *me encierro a llorar.* [38]

If he triumphs in the duel he could be jailed, *puesto a la sombra*; and if he lost, he would be dead at the hands of his adversary. And that dilemma is the reason why he can't face the situation, because either way he would lose the woman who has won his heart.

---

[37] Yesterday, from being scared to kill/ instead of fighting/ I started to run

[38] I saw myself in jail or dead/ I thought of not seeing you and I trembled.../ And I who never shied away from/ the night, in anguish/ I lock myself away to cry.

Gardel performing in Paris.

Tango singer in Paris (1928-1929)

With his baggage of tangos and guitarists in hand, Gardel disembarked in Barcelona. He proceeded with a trip in the Graham Paige to Toulouse with his personal chauffeur Antonio Sumage, "the Aviator", behind the wheel. At the Villa Rosa, he caught a brief glimpse of his French relatives, and then continued en route to Paris. His agent in France, Luis Pierotti, had reached an agreement with Paul Santolini, the kingpin of Parisian nightlife, that opened the door for Gardel to work in theaters and cabarets. This entrepreneur was known as "the Napoleon of Montmare" for his wide-ranging control and power over the show business world.

The tango had already established its credentials as a music and dance style in Paris around the threshold of the 20th century. However, the tango-song was a new development, still unknown

Un grand gala au profit des sinistrés de la Guadeloupe

Nous avons annoncé ici-même le gala qui doit avoir lieu dimanche soir au théâtre Femina pour la présentation au public parisien de la célèbre

Carlos Gardel

vedette sud-Américaine, le créateur de tous les tangos à la mode : Carlos Gardel.

Voici le télégramme que vient de recevoir M. Paul Santo organisateur de cette manifestation artistique.

Barcelone 26/9

Paul Santo, 6, rue Fontaine, Paris.

« Serais désireux consentiez que concert de présentation théâtre Femina soit donné au bénéfice des sinistrés de la Guadeloupe et passiez ainsi de mes débuts en France un geste fraternel qui me tient à cœur.

« Amitiés : Gardel. »

Bien entendu, M. Paul Santo a immédiatement tenu à s'associer au joli geste du grand artiste et versera la totalité des bénéfices de la soirée de dimanche au comité de secours aux sinistrés de la Guadeloupe.

Paris fêtera comme il convient Carlos Gardel qui est une des gloires théâtrales de l'Amérique du Sud et qui vient de prouver une fois de plus qu'il est aussi un homme de cœur.

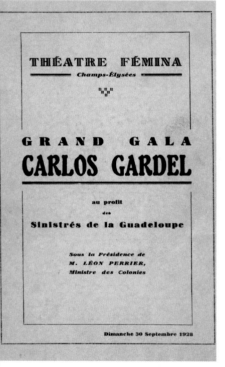

THÉATRE FÉMINA
——— Champs-Élysées ———

GRAND GALA
CARLOS GARDEL

au profit
des
Sinistrés de la Guadeloupe

Sous la Présidence de
M. LÉON PERRIER,
Ministre des Colonies

Dimanche 30 Septembre 1928

One of several articles
announcing his debut in Paris,
and the program cover.

in France. There were *Orquestas Típicas* working steadily there and Francisco Canaro enjoyed a big hit in 1925, but it was the music for inspiring the dance that was praised so enthusiastically. At most, there might be some chorus in the middle of the piece. What Gardel contributes at that moment had never been seen before. Tangos sung in Spanish (with the translation of some lyrics distributed with the program) with guitar accompaniment. Obviously, all the melody was going to be in the voice, a voice that struggled in reinforcing its qualities with the lyrical content since the Parisian audience neither knew nor sang along with the lyrics.

The first event was at the Fémina Theater, a benefit performance for the victims of floods on the Island of Guadaloupe, at that time a French overseas possession. The tango orchestra of Manuel Pizarro, a string orchestra, and the jazz band of León Abbey all performed. Gardel with his guitarists was the star attraction of the night. Dressed as gauchos, they employed their standard practice of the guitarists making their entrance on stage first to perform a pair of instrumental songs. Then the singer joined them. The audience response was so extraordinary after the initial anticipation that Gardel, off in the wings, would say to his chauffeur:

- "But che, are we in Paris or Buenos Aires?"

The next day, October 1, 1928, the singer sent a telegram to his partner José Razzano: "Last night I performed at the Fémina Theater, enormous success. Love to all. Hugs. Carlos".

After the performance at the Theater would come a series of performances at the Cabaret Florida, located at Rue Clichy 20. The impresario Paul Santolini had decorated the cabaret, even including paintings with images and motifs of the Pampas among the fountains, swans and mirrors. There were numerous clients of the rich Argentina of that era and the Florida became a meeting point for South American magnates and diplomats. In that way Santolini successfully attracted the legions of rioplatense

Gardel in Paris with the Torterolo brothers and other friends.

millionaires who in turn had the chance to present the premier performers of the national art to their friends and acquaintances in the French capital. These were three months of tremendous importance for this style only recently arrived in Paris. The name of Carlos Gardel stood out on the illuminated posters of the cabaret. The show business press raved about it. In a telegram to José Razzano, Gardel declared: "I continue triumphing. Consider me the *vedette*[39] of the current scene. A big hit. Regards. Like back there, I'm raising the dead". The final phrase was referring to his compatriots who were down on their luck and came to ask him for help or, in criollo, *gauchadas*. His performances at the cabaret were preceded by a sextet playing tangos, big bands playing jazz and tropical rhythms so the people in attendance would dance. Meanwhile, he celebrated his 38th birthday on December 11 at the Eiffel Tower restaurant among fellow musicians and his new

---

[39] Vedette: the female dancers, especially the featured performers, at famed Parisian nightspots like the Folies Bergere and Moulin Rouge of the era. Gardel is gender-joking with Defino here by calling himself the "leading lady" of Parisian nightlife.

friends and acquaintances in Paris.

He informed his partner in Buenos Aires by letter:

"My record sales are fantastic. In three months, they sold 70,000 copies: they're scared and didn't have enough to meet the demand. The famous magazine 'La Rouse' that comes out at this time of year with a deluxe year-end issue will have my photo in color on the cover. You'll also see the record catalogs in Paris that I'm sending you have my photo on the cover. It's good to land on your feet... Right now, I'm preparing to sing in the Paris Opera House, the one we talked about so much since we were kids. Who would have thought 16 years ago that I would make it to sing at the Opera House in front of all the big shot dignitaries, from the President of the Republic and his ministers on down"?

Indeed, on February 5, 1929, the famous *Bal des Petits Lits Blancs* (Ball of the Little White Beds) festival featuring performances by Maurice Chevalier, Henry Garot, Mistinguet and Lucienne Boyer was held at the sumptuous Paris Opera House. Gardel sang there, "The King of Tango", as the French called him. Amidst a standing ovation that blended hearty applause with enthusiastic exclamations, the audience twice demanded repeat performances of *El Carretero*, a song written by Arturo de Nava. It was his definitive breakthrough. The Osvaldo Fresedo Tango Orchestra shared the ovations for the performance that night, although they were not quite as thunderous. You have to imagine the Paris of that period. Beneath the surface sheen of styles and fashions, traditions, political meetings of all kinds, the atmosphere of the time throbbed with the pulse of an all-encompassing party. The city was triumphantly living the life of the capital of the avant gardes, the victor in World War I. To triumph there meant you had reached the epicenter of fame and renown.

From Paris, Gardel dropped down to the French Riviera, a frequent destination for the wealthy from around the world. He sang at the Cannes Casino there and, according to several sources, at parties either attended or hosted by Sally Wakefield, the daughter of a British tobacco magnate who would later invest in the French films featuring Gardel.

His schedule brought him back to Paris for two weeks as the headliner at the Empire Theater. There is an amusing anecdote from the journalist Edmundo Guibourg, who happened to be in Paris and went looking for his childhood friend Carlos Gardel because Jacinto Benavente wanted to invite him to dinner. The reasons? The friendliness and admiration the singer had awakened in the writer in Buenos Aires, who indicated his profound interest in knowing about the different forms of *lunfardo:*

> "When their meal was over, Benavente very enthusiastically expressed to Gardel the linguistic importance contained in the words of his songs. You can imagine the satisfaction the singer felt over that. He didn't miss the opportunity to tell me, very pleased with himself: "Look at that, and I always thought I was just a singer. Now it turns out that I'm a linguist, too."

In Paris, he continued recording discs and started a new season at the Cabaret Florida. From there, he traveled to Spain for a fourth tour to perform in honor of the masses during the theater seasons in Barcelona and Madrid.

According to Gardel himself and his tour companions, the general success was overwhelming on various fronts. He sold thousands of records and performed on internationally famous stages, while the possibility of filming movies with Paramount Studios began to take shape.

Before the group returned to Buenos Aires, José Ricardo, the guitarist who had accompanied Gardel since 1917, decided to leave the ensemble to start a musical career in Europe with his brother Rafael Ricardo. In addition to the previously mentioned recordings with Gardel, some instrumental songs by the trio of guitarists remained behind in Paris.

A season in Buenos Aires, 1929-1930

Back in Buenos Aires, Gardel returned to the home he bought for his mother, Berta Gardes. He was the *rioplatense* artist who enjoyed the greatest international fame. People recognized him in the street. People remember that when he walked into some halls, all it took was a slight nod of his head for everyone there to feel greeted. By that time, his life and work were an object of permanent curiosity, to the point that the most traditional Argentinean daily newspaper, *La Nación*, published a report on Gardel's daily life:

"The house is low, old, and not particularly symmetrical in its layout. Perhaps much of the blame lies with the still recent arrival of the artist and the constant traveling required in his world. But from what we have seen, compare: How different it is from what we imagined! A hall, actually more like a patio, big, cold, with three guitars, two travel trunks, a phonograph and a pair of very high boots, maybe because that style will appear more criollo in Europe. On the dining room table, nothing but white clothes and other garments strewn about in colorful disarray. And the bedroom of the artist, you know what it's like? A furnished room but very modest, with a small narrow bronze bed. On the wall, no artists, no film heroines, no admirers. Several austere family portraits of respectable ancestors who look like working men and watch seriously over him as he sleeps. On seeing Carlitos, healthy, young, not worried about a thing, flooding every place he enters with "Venice Carnival" style, you imagine that he lives a life of leisure and must dedicate 24 hours of every day to spending (his fame for being generous is legendary) all the money that falls from the sky on him. And, nevertheless, you see how different it is. His life is leisurely, certainly, he spends money, enjoys himself, goes for walks, and gives every impression of being a happy man. What you don't know, what you don't even suspect, is how much he works during the hours when he is out of the public eye:

"The people don't really assume that I work. They believe that I make money without doing anything. And I do earn it, that's true, I make a lot of money, but I also work many hours every day. This figure should be enough to make them realize that: I record up to 20 songs a month now. In addition to the actual recording, which has to be daily when you're doing that many songs, you have to count the rehearsals, deciding on the instrumentation, coordinating and blending the guitars, the changes that always have to be introduced so the singing and instruments blend smoothly, and there you'll have a picture of what my life is like. It's very nice, I can't complain, but it is continuous work".

There are plenty of interviews in daily newspapers and magazines during this period. Gardel talks about horses and discs, about the movies he will make in France, and future tours of Great Britain, Germany and Russia. He makes jokes and tells funny stories until the late-night hours, and to a bunch of football fans in the stands when the game gets boring. He continues his physical training with demanding exercise workouts. He speaks simply and tells anecdotes that show an intent to take stock. He demystifies the myths surrounding his meeting with Razzano and is quite consistent about the mischievousness of including tangos, a universal passport in his repertoire. He is grateful for the small, simple things in life. But there are also walls where he grows more guarded, when journalists ask questions like: Is your voice still the same? How does it feel singing without Razzano? How old are you? Will you stay in the country? How do they view us overseas? How does your body feel? Are there any signs of decline? Do you miss Buenos Aires? Do you like women? What country are you from? What are Spanish women, French women, English women, North American women, and women with their heads in the cloud like? He has to improvise and invent a character for replying to even the most outlandish curiosities. Generally, the answer he invents comes out good-natured, amusing and generous. Although on one occasion, according to Aníbal Troilo, he said:

"Get him out. You don't have to stir up idiots because afterwards they make you out to be a debtor or cheater".

When he speaks in this period, he reveals something of that rare capacity to transform himself, of representing the multiple facets of the world he knew and experienced in the tangos he sang. Commenting on his origins, he doesn't shy away from voicing observations and reflections that were above all intuitions, ideas that had recently flowered but still had not fully matured. He thinks as he creates, as he performs and records discs, of what to do with his future, how to go beyond himself within the context of human limitations. He embodies his destiny, outlining how to make it happen by being true to himself.

On December 31, 1929, after five years of not recording with Razzano, he cut two sides with him that will be the last two made by the duo.

He incorporated the guitar of Ángel Domingo Riverol into his group in early 1930. He continued his appearances in Buenos Aires, the Argentinean provinces and Montevideo, and recording with that ensemble accompanying him. In April of that year, he successfully tried out adding Rodolfo Biagi on piano and Antonio Rodio on violin for his recording sessions. Later, he would record a handful of very beautiful pieces with Francisco Canaro's Orchestra. Some of them are found in the first sound film made in Argentina, "Encuadre de Canciones", directed by Eduardo Morera. Today it is recognized as an indispensable testament to the highly advanced ideas of the era. Gardel sings in front of the

1930: Gardel is filmed singing various songs.

cameras and engages in conversation with some of his favorite composers, including Flores, Discépolo, Arturo de Nava and Canaro. His destiny also lies in the songs on the movie theater screens that are multiplying around the country. He was filmed singing in his native Argentina before the movies scheduled to be shot in Paris.

The private side

We already indicated once he settled into his international fame as the leading tango singer, his private life and habits were observed in minute detail. More often than not, he found himself in trouble trying to provide answers to incisive journalists "looking for that special note". Reading his statements in the press we can already observe how, little by little, he uses clever, ingenious ways of answering without saying much of anything, or gives evasive answers without showing any disinterest in the interview. It is also true that with so much committed to paper, you end up recognizing a profile of the character traits defining his personality. If these materials are significant, no less so are the memories referred to by the substantial number of people who dealt with him. To know Gardel, to have dealt with him or shared some situation with him, meant having a relationship with the most famous tango artist and, coming full circle, enjoying his generosity and hospitality.

There are constant factors running throughout his life and they are outlined in the importance of his mother. Above all starting in 1917-1918, when the son was able to have his mother retire, but still provide her with a good life within the simple, modest tastes that characterized Berta's lifestyle. Much like in his teenage years, Gardel was periodically absent from Buenos Aires. He went out to party hearty with his friends, off to the racetracks, or that typical circle that brought men together then, finishing off those days at home, dead tired from the lavish spending and wild carousing in nightclubs. It was common to find Gardel surrounded by friends, all of them dedicated to the activity and joy of living life to the fullest. There was always laughter, jokes, and outbursts of partying in the time they shared together. At the end of his wandering, he returned to his mother's house, who spent her time dedicated to following the career of her son as best she could. He in turn said of her:

"... The most delicious stew made by her hands is more delicious and worth more than the most expensive dishes of the best hotels in the world... The applause of the audience is very nice, but what are they worth compared to one 'You sang well' from my mother?"

Gardel was a man of his times and it would be foolish to try and look at him through the filter of present-day models, just as it would be to stigmatize some things contained in the lyrics of tangos by isolating them from the changing society in which they were written. He was born without a father who acknowledged him and, of course, it was no secret to him that the emigration and the tenacious determination of his mother was directly related to his existence. A constant, permanent concern for her well-being is evident throughout the artist's entire career. This despite the fact his escapades seriously annoyed her any number of times, especially during his teenage and younger years, when he had to deceive her about where he was going... Or that occasion when he was shot on the left side of the chest. People remember the warning that Gardel gave to the friends who were going to go accompany Berta to the hospital:

"Araca... la jaevi, ¡la jaevi!... Fue un yobaca... ¿manyás? Un yobaca". [Careful, the Vieja[40]! It was a horse, you understand? A horse].

It's a sure thing that he engaged in this practice of hiding

---

[40] Vieja: an affectionate term of endearment widely used by most Argentineans when referring to their mother.

physical discomfort or other problems from her on other matters. The relationship with Isabel Martínez del Valle, the longest one that Gardel maintained, went through a difficult period because Berta did not look kindly on it, perhaps because the young girl was only 14 years old compared to Carlos' 29 when they started seeing each other. Letters from Gardel and comments from friends indicate the mother didn't look favorably on that situation. However, it is recognized that both women later shared the triumphs and news of the man who was away from the two of them. After the accident in Medellín, they bonded together in their sorrow, and went together to the cemetery. Nonetheless, we know there were periods of serious complications for Gardel, prompted by pressure from Isabel's family to obtain economic support without having to pay him back. (Did they sell their silence about the age difference?). We believe this situation formed one part of the various concerns that the son tried to shield his mother from, like the friction with Razzano caused by the latter's poor administration of Gardel's business affairs.

According to accounts of several people close to him, Carlos Gardel, along with being ready and willing to have a good time with his friends, also experienced occasional moments when he kept to himself and was depressed. Sometimes when he was in a bad mood, he isolated himself in the midst of the revelry, his mind drifting off as he retreated deep inside himself.

Gardel in films (1931)

It has been repeated over and over how important films were in projecting Gardel as an artist and star. However, for anyone who knows his recorded work in depth, the films contribute reasons worth praising, but one typically prefers going back to his discs from force of habit. Why? Because with Gardel, his voice is the foundation... and as far as the images are concerned, a few will often suffice. We occasionally go to see the films, but the constant

Gardel (seated, center) with his idol Charlie Chaplin
to his left at a party in Nice.

Paris 1931: A very happy Carlos Gardel smiles for the camera
the day he signed his first contract with Paramount Pictures.
With him are his manager Luis Pierotti, Florián Rey and
reporter José Luis Salado.

we return to is listening to his records, with his smiling face greeting us on the covers.

People in Buenos Aires had been advised he would go to Paris to make films. Most likely the success Al Jolson enjoyed from singing in movies led Gardel to think along those lines for his career. In December 1930, he embarked once again for Europe to perform again at the Empire Theater in Paris with his guitarists Barbieri, Aguilar and Riverol. They traveled on the *Conte Rosso*, where they shared the voyage with the cast of the Teatro Sarmiento revue company, and directors Manuel Romero and Bayón Herrera. Apparently, they talked with Gardel about his possibilities for screen success during the trip.

Following the performances in the French capital, the famed *chanteur argentin* went on to Nice, the ever-popular destination of millionaires and international artists. He sang at the Mediterranean Casino there and participated in the parties that Madame Wakefield, a patron of artists, gave at her castle eight

Carlos Gardel in "Luces de Buenos Aires" (1931)

kilometers outside Nice. In that private setting, there were some shared scenes with Gardel singing and Chaplin improvising comic sketches.

One time the jockey Ireneo Leguisamo was invited by his good friend Carlos Gardel to join the party. In his memoir he comments:

> "I arrived on the French Riviera in an era when this coastal region of extraordinary beauty brought together the international elite: kings, princes, lords of industry and banking. They were all drawn by the vision of the Mediterranean Casino, the Monte Carlo Casino and the whole spectacle of an ostentatious era. Before that audience, our Zorzal shined bright with his unmistakable image and exceptional artistic talent".

Mistinguet, Maurice Chevalier and Gregor Kalikian were among the artists who performed on the Nice stage in that era. Gardel included some French songs in his repertoire there that were warmly appreciated by the audiences. At the same time, he was increasing the number of tangos he performed. These were the tangos he then recorded in Paris after returning there with Barbieri and Riverol, following the disagreement with Aguilar that prompted his early departure back to Buenos Aires.

In the French capital, they continued with their plans to make the projected film with a tango theme. They found director Adelqui Millar, who was then working at the studios Paramount had set up in Joinville to produce films in different languages. The negotiations moved ahead until they concluded in a contract stipulating that Gardel would star as the main character in a script to be written by Manuel Romero and Bayón Herrera. The cast for the movie would be made up of actors and actresses from the previously mentioned Teatro Sarmiento company who were in Paris. The orchestra of Julio de Caro would perform part of the score.

The title for the first of the important series of films that would bring Gardel to the silver screen was "Luces de Buenos Aires" ("Lights of Buenos Aires"). He sang two songs in the movie, *Tomo y Obligo*, a tango whose music he wrote himself, and *El Rosal*, by Matos Rodríguez and Romero. The plot was simple and built on the local flavor of many tango lyrics. A rural landowner, also a singer, amateur guitar player and womanizer, is left behind by a young girl who heads for the bright lights and theaters of Buenos Aires to start her career as an actress. The man can't live with his sorrow and goes to search for her, only to be on the receiving end of her scorn. He returns to the country full of sadness over the life she is being dragged down into. But all is not lost, because two gaucho workers from his farm "will steal her" from the theater and bring her to him. The "abduction" takes place in an odd scene in which the gauchos, who bought their tickets for a balcony of the theater, get the idea of lassoing her with the lariat they use to capture animals in the fields. They hoist the lassoed lady up to the balcony and, amidst all the tumult and commotion amongst the cast and audience, escape with the woman to take her back to their boss. They find him at the foot of a dried-out rose bush, sadly singing the pledge of love that she had left behind. This degrading episode of the "lassoing of women" is a forerunner of other famous scenes in film history. We can recall the film "Bus Stop" in 1956, in which the cowboy Don Murray lassos Marilyn Monroe just as she is about to escape his unwanted harassment in a bus. Also in the film "Indiana Jones and the Temple of Doom", Harrison Ford lassos Kate Capshaw to draw her towards him and give her the kiss of the well-known Hollywood happy ending.

The best-remembered piece by Gardel in Luces de Buenos Aires is *Tomo y Obligo*, a tango whose theme certainly fits in the classic vein, where the deceived man drowns his sorrows in wine over finding himself betrayed and slurs insults against women. There is one juicy detail about his performance in the film. Gardel, who apparently felt that more rehearsals were needed before the final filming of the scene, was abruptly summoned to the set and was still very upset when he performed. Nevertheless, he sang such a memorable version of the song that, in film theaters in Spain and the Americas, the audiences forced the projectionists to rewind the film and repeat the scene where Gardel performs *Tomo y Obligo* on screen in a seaside tavern at the port. The essence of the finale shows him saying:

Siga un consejo... no se enamore
y si una vuelta le toca hocicar,
fuerza, canejo, sufra y no llore
que un hombre macho no debe llorar. [41]

As he finishes the final line, he covers his face to conceal his unrestrained sobbing.

While he was filming *Luces de Buenos Aires*, Gardel had to perform in the *Parades des Femmes revue*, "headlining a cast of 100 artists of both sexes", as the newspapers announced. On May 23 the daily newspaper Le Figaro commented:

"This great artist, known and admired in all of Paris, has made a triumphal return in the sensational revue... whose success has been hailed far and wide in the press".

He stayed in France until August of that year, 1931. In the few hours of leisure time he had, Gardel went to the cabarets in the company of Sally Baron Wakefield and her husband George. Among the stops was the Pigalle, owned by his friend, the bandoneon player and conductor Manuel Pizarro. He also went out to the Longchamp racetrack and walked the streets of Paris with Julio de Caro.

Maybe the friendship between Gardel and De Caro merits special mention. Why De Caro? The history of tango singles out De Caro as the great architect of its definitive structure, the musician who transformed the tango into a music written and interpreted by arrangements that gave each bandleader an

---

[41] Take my advice... don't fall in love/ And if some turn smothers you in kisses/ Strength, *canejo*, suffer and don't cry/ A real man (macho) must not cry

individual style. He was nine years younger than Gardel but his birthday was also December 11. He was born in a home next door to the music conservatory directed by his father, José de Caro. His entrance into the world of tango, curiously enough, happened at the same time as Gardel. Gardel with his vocal creativity and Julio de Caro as a violin player in the major orchestras of the late 1910s and early 1920s. After that, De Caro would be the composer and director of the most important orchestra of the 1920s: the *Sexteto Típico*, with which de Caro traveled to Europe to perform in France, Italy and Great Britain. He was together with Gardel in the Mediterranean Casino of Nice, ready to perform, when his stage fright momentarily got the better of him and delayed the beginning of the performance. De Caro himself recounts in his memoir:

> "At that moment a voice in French could be heard coming from the audience, requesting a moment of silence: 'Ladies and gentlemen, I expressly traveled from Paris to this wonderful French Riviera, this time not to admire the scenery, but to accompany my compatriot on the night of his debut performance here. He is a great interpreter of the Argentinean tango who, as I do, will offer the best of his spirit in the music. And since you have already given me a round of applause, I ask of you another round of applause for Julio de Caro'. Once the speech was finished and with my eyes now accustomed to the harsh glare from the spotlights, I could make out Carlos Gardel, standing at the side of his far distant table..."

Of course, this gesture of support would have weighed heavily on the musician's decision when they urged him to perform the music for the *Luces de Buenos Aires* film. He would choose that project at the expense of his commitment to perform in England for King George V.

The tradition has rewarded the two friends by celebrating December 11 as International Tango Day.

Buenos Aires again

The return of Carlos Gardel to his home country in August 1931 was a major event that prompted much activity from producers and journalists. Augusto Álvarez, manager of the Cine-Teatro Broadway in Buenos Aires, waited for the singer at the port of Montevideo to get the jump on his competitors in hiring him. When Gardel first set foot in Buenos Aires, he had already signed contracts to perform. The following day the *La Razón* and *La Jornada* daily newspapers both published interviews. In those stories, Gardel was exultant over his latest projects, presenting himself as a film star who soon must return to Europe where "he has signed contracts for more movies".

- "What memory do you bring back from Europe?"
- "Paris! Paris honored me with its admiration and applause. It feels my songs as if they were French. The city has developed a deep affection for our popular music, one like no other".

He sang at the Broadway with his trio of guitars, since he had just incorporated Domingo Julio Vivas into his ensemble of stringed instruments. He also played with them on the *Casa América* radio station in performances that promoted the *Bodegas Giol*. Tireless, he made recordings with his three guitarists, Gregor Kalikian and the orchestra of Francisco Canaro (maybe among the best he ever did with this band leader). After that, he crossed the Río de la Plata to perform at theaters in Montevideo, where an enthusiastic Uruguayan audience awaited him. He returned to Buenos Aires to add more recordings for his record label *Odeón*, before departing for Europe once again, this time without his backing musicians.

It's worth our while to stop and consider Gardel's two-month *rioplatense* residency. We point out that this marked his transformation into a film star both at that moment and his future plans. He wasn't only announcing projects to film in France, but also in the United States.

People remarked on his habits and eccentricities. For example, his habit of drawing and writing with his left hand even though he was right-handed. He would take advantage of the question they would ask about that, something that generally happened, to build up his image. He replied that he used the left hand to write the dedication to the people for whom he held greater affection. In short, banalities valued by the so-called gossip magazines, or those closely related to them. It was also during this period when he declared that he liked "all songs, even if they're Japanese if they're beautiful,", his own words aimed at defending himself from the scathing attacks of criollo chauvinism, who imagined a watered-down version in this international Carlos Gardel who had included French and Italian language songs in his performances at the Cine-Teatro Broadway. Nor was the singer intimidated by the criticism (despite the familiar bitterness) and recorded them with Gregor Kalikian's orchestra when it landed in Buenos Aires for a period of time. Kalikian also took advantage of any opportunity he had to praise and defend Gardel:

> "It would be appropriate to condemn him if he would sing French versions of criollo tangos. But Gardel has known how to choose lovely and highly regarded Parisian ballads, aspiring with that, we can be certain, to tell his story and expand his repertoire in the manner necessary for achieving the category of international singer".

As for his love of the ponies and going to the races, Gardel claims that he has horses at the track but doesn't bet, a declaration disproved by the facts on various occasions. Later, he would even place bets by telegram from New York.

Meanwhile, in September of 1931, he did the radio performance of *Bodegas Giol*, singing a tango obviously for publicity purposes despite his evident distaste for doing it. Apparently, he was influenced by the desire to save the job of a friend responsible for the program's creative design. During that period, there were still no clear guidelines about the scope and limits of use of popular personality in advertising, although Gardel undoubtedly was headed for abuse for propaganda purposes to promote a certain image people wanted to give of Argentina. Alongside the sincere display of his photos in the homes of common people, restaurants, and buses, there are the slogans of the State. In the early 1960s, a renowned legend who attempted to inspire hope with dubious nationalist options said next to a photo of Gardel with his well-known smile. "Buy YPF gas, so that Carlitos won't cry".

The question of sharing his earnings 50-50 with his partner Razzano, now definitively an ex-working partner, were going though bad times that threatened to become irreversible. Razzano formed part of powerful guild interests that asserted themselves then and again years later, when they argued and recovered the rights to inheritance of Gardel's body of work. It was during that period, the two months alluded to before, when Gardel initiated his commitments with Armando Defino to administer his economic affairs.

In the artistic sphere, although his status as the leading tango singer was unquestioned in Argentina and Europe, a certain animus circulated, surely fueled by other singers (or who once were), to undermine his prestige and fame. It is well-known that fame often carries dangers with it, dangers that go hand-in-hand with an overexposed image in the eyes of the public. He was criticized for including foreign material and other songs in his repertoire, his fashion style and stage presence, his frequent absences from Buenos Aires, etc. Along with journalistic and everyday world concerns, he ran into jealousies, rivals, rejections. There were remarks that pointed to another, now-forgotten singer named Santiago Devin as a rival who surpassed Gardel as the popular favorite. Despite the enormous amount of money he earned, he was in the red financially. Even more, he was forced to request an accounting of income and general withdrawals from his Odeón label account in light of a strong suspicion that his partner had withdrawn money as an advance against future recordings. As for his shiny new move into the world of sound movies, not everyone approved of the effort. There were those who thought that, by taking a national product but making the films in France and later the United States, Gardel was diluting his talent and squandering the potential opportunity of making a truly national cinema using Argentinean directors and the homegrown film industry.

With all those things and other situations that complicated his life with new developments, enigmas, and surely emotions, Carlos Gardel decided to travel to Europe by himself. No doubt one of his main objectives was to pin down the specific steps required to pursue the movie career he had started. He needed to deal with Paramount in depth, during a time when the movie business was not exactly flourishing. There is speculation he was also concerned over aspects connected to improvements necessary to moving his career forward: techniques related to diction and singing, command of languages, etc. Even more, he was always diligent about the need to adapt the screenplays and supporting cast of actors to the realities of the *rioplatense* scenes that were central to the plots of his films.

New films in Paris (1932)

Gardel needed to be alone and used the ocean waters as the vehicle. With the maturity of being 40 years old, the insecurity over the future of his voice and the new horizons opened up by the movie world, he felt a change of course was drawing closer. But who could he talk with about these things? With who? Someone else from over there in Buenos Aires, who would have roots like his own and hold a similar life story in their hands? Not in literature, not in sports or politics, not in any other artistic styles, no one had emerged from Argentina with these growing international prospects as Gardel had. Not even his musical colleagues De Caro, Canaro, Fresedo, etc., had individually reached his level of originality. They were all far away from attaining that. Even more, that same country of Argentina that imagined itself so great, was now showing serious indications of fragility caused by the crisis of 1930, the institutional breakdown of its political system, and a halt to the immigration that until that point had marked the base of its solid prosperity.

Carlos Gardel with Imperio Argentina in "Melodía de Arrabal"

Gardel had to think in terms of planning his career for the future, probably still without a clear awareness of what those issues involved, but certainly of that charged atmosphere affecting the different environments wherever he looked. He decided to go away from Buenos Aires for a couple of months and ended up being absent for 14. He left without guitarists, assistants, or producers. He went above all to study his potential in the film world. Not too much documentation exists of his whereabouts in that period, unlike with other journeys, but the letters sent to Armando Defino, the man who became his new agent, are revealing. He recorded in Barcelona backed by musicians who had never appeared in his public career until then. There were radio broadcasts from Paris connected with Buenos Aires and other capital cities. He initiated a relationship with poet Alfredo Le Pera, who became his screenwriter from that point on, with both men involved in choosing the songs, plots and actors of his films. In an extraordinary achievement, between September and November of 1932, he filmed *Espérame, Melodía de Arrabal* and the short *La Casa es Seria* at the Paramount studio in Joinville. The last two featured Imperio Argentina as the female co-star and found Carlos Gardel playing two different roles in each film. He had raised part of the financing for the film thanks to the good graces of Sally Wakefield and her husband.

Carlos Gardel is the creator of the most famous tangos of his career from those films. One of them is *Silencio*, from *Melodía de Arrabal*. Its lyric anticipates the plot line of the 1998 Steven Spielberg mega-production "Saving Private Ryan" almost 70 years later.

The tango *Silencio* tells a moving story whose inspiration is undoubtedly familiar to many homes that experienced World War I or any similar large-scale conflict:

Silencio en la noche, ya todo está en calma,
el músculo duerme, la ambición descansa. [42]

A mother rocks the cradle in which she reared her five sons, her hopes. They grow up and now they are five sons who march off to the shop to work. But once again there is:

Silencio en la noche, ya todo está en calma,
el músculo duerme, la ambición trabaja... [43]

When ambition works, it changes the story. The events that will lead to the catastrophe for this family are triggered. The ambition works...

Un clarín se oye... peligra la patria...
y al grito de guerra los hombres se matan,

---

[42] Silence in the night, everything is calm now/ The muscle sleeps, ambition rests
[43] Silence in the night, everything is calm now/ The muscle sleeps, ambition is working

cubriendo de sangre los campos de Francia. [44]

The same site of France is also chosen by Steven Spielberg to locate the action of his film. The drama also revolves around the death of brothers in the war (in this case World War II) that leaves a North American mother alone, which makes the high command of the army sensitive to the situation. They order the search for private Ryan at the front in an attempt to keep the mother from ending up alone.

In the tango *Silencio*, after the battles in which the soldier sons die:

Hoy todo ha pasado, renacen las plantas...
un himno a la vida los arados cantan.
Y la viejecita de canas muy blancas
se quedó muy sola, con cinco medallas
que por cinco héroes le premió la patria. [45]

In the silence of the night, after the war, the passion rests, so that the hopes are reborn. Now it is not just a single mother but a chorus of mothers who are rocking the cradles of their sons.

Silencio en la noche... ya todo está en calma.
el músculo duerme... la ambición descansa.
Un coro lejano de madres que cantan,
mecen en sus cunas nuevas esperanzas. [46]

The story certainly rings true to life and it is so effective for that

---

[44] A bugle sounds...the country is in danger/ And hearing the war cry, the men kill each other/ covering the fields of France in blood

[45] Today it's all over, the plants are blooming again.../ The plows sing a hymn to life/ And the little old woman with very white hair/ is left very lonely, with five medals/ for five heroes the country awarded her

[46] Silence in the night... everything is calm now/ The muscle sleeps... ambition rests/ A distant chorus of mothers who are singing/ rocking new hopes in their cradles

very reason. In wartime, it is more common for them to return the medals recalling the dead, as described in the tango *Silencio*, than those odd decisions of the North American high command to save an anonymous life, one among hundreds of thousands of soldiers. Although these plot lines wouldn't echo as strongly now in present-day wars, since the thousands of dead belong to the civilian population. Now wars are possible where one adversary can calculate its professional troops will not suffer any losses in battle.

The climax of the tango says:

Silencio en la noche... silencio en las almas. [47]

That turns out to be similar to the verses that begin and successively develop and detail the *raison d'etre* of the poem, although the finishing touch of this final verse is the silence extended to the souls. Undoubtedly a reminder of the irreparable consequences ambition produces when it works.

With this piece, a collaboration with Alfredo Le Pera and Horacio Pettorossi, Carlos Gardel sang an anti-war tango. It did not go unnoticed that it paid tribute to the people of the country where he was born. The film version of this tango in *Melodía de Arrabal* is excellent, although the no less magnificent recorded versions waxed in Buenos Aires are much better known by a wide margin.

Last return to Buenos Aires (1932-1933)

The confession Gardel made to Defino in a letter was gradually being fulfilled:

---

[47] Silence in the night... silence in the souls.

"I'm staying here!. I have to make movies. I don't want to lie around getting a suntan on the beaches, I don't want to sing any more there...".

At the end of December 1932, he arrived at the port of Buenos Aires carrying all his cinematic baggage mentioned before, to put his economic and personal affairs in order, record discs and get reacquainted with close friends. On December 31, while praising his willingness to do the interview, the reporters from *La Nación* remarked:

> "And you don't have to wait long for the replies to come from this forever young gentleman, for whom traveling appears to rejuvenate the spirit due to the change in viewpoints and outlooks he finds in different countries and peoples".

The reunions in Buenos Aires brought together his closest friends from the racetrack, tango and theater worlds, and some journalists. However, the disputes with his ex-duo partner José Razzano were not resolved. It reached the point where Gardel revoked the contract naming Razzano as general manager of his assets that he had signed seven years before in 1925. He immediately named Armando Defino as the person in charge of his business affairs.

Guitarist Horacio Pettorossi returned to Buenos Aires with him, an Argentinean musician who previously led tango orchestras during his extended stays in Europe. He would later travel to Europe again and the United States accompanying Gardel. The singer's appearances in Buenos Aires incorporated Pettorossi into his ensemble of guitars, and you can also hear his presence on the songs Gardel recorded during that period.

His performances got an enthusiastic reception from his friends and the press alike. The daily newspaper *Crítica* wrote:

> "His appearance is the same, but his soul hasn't changed one bit,

either. He is always the same young guy free of vanity and envy, all sincere smiles, a friend of his friends who makes them love him from the start and forever".

Later, when they ask him his reason for returning to Buenos Aires, he replies very decisively:

- "I'm coming for one year. I'll record the songs from the movies I just finished filming in Joinville here. During this time, I'll appear before my old audience again".
- "And after that? The French Riviera again?"
- "No, after that straight to Hollywood".

His stay lasted for 11 months as he went back to enjoying his well-known habits. He arrived on December 30 and celebrated New Year's Eve the following day with his mother and friends. On January 1, 1933, he went to the racetrack. He started an extensive series of recording sessions on January 13 that would last until November. He was backed by his quartet of guitars, the Orchestra of Alberto Castellanos (his new musical collaborator in Paris and New York), and Francisco Canaro. He recorded the songs from his recent movies, titles written by friends of proven loyalty and skill as lyricists. He also did new versions of songs recorded years before, sometimes singing a duo with himself.

One series of performances among his many tours of cities in the interior of Argentina and Uruguay illuminates his capacity for innovation. On March 24, 1933, he appeared in a theatrical show named *De Gabino a Gardel* (From Gabino to Gardel). The title accurately refers to a journey through Argentinean music from folkloric sounds to the tango. The audience response was overwhelmingly enthusiastic when he sang his new tangos, *Melodía de Arrabal* and *Silencio* as well as now-classic songs like *Mano a Mano* and *El Carretero*. The daily newspaper *La Nación* emphasized that Carlos Gardel's presence was the highlight of the evening at the Teatro Nacional. Another newspaper, *El Mundo*,

Two images from the Silva photo session in Montevideo, 1933.
The José Silva photos are widely considered
to be the best Gardel photos.

His smile, the elegant, charming feature that
distinguished him from other artists of the era.

Farewell party in Buenos Aires, 1933. Gardel (seated, center) with Ireneo Leguisamo to his left and the Edgardo Donato orchestra.

made an observation that still applies in our own times:

> "The tango collects distinctive nuances through each interpreter that transform it, naturally, according to each temperament. But they always reflect a marked tendency toward that accent so particular to Gardel, and it is impossible for other singers to separate themselves from his influence".

Carlos Gardel again participated in benefit concerts, as he customarily did, performing alongside tango orchestras and the jazz big bands enjoying increased popularity in Argentina at the time. He sang again alongside old touring companions like Roberto Firpo, Francisco Canaro and Osvaldo Fresedo. Leading actors and singers, including fundamental figures in Argentina from that period like the Magaldi-Noda duo, Mercedes Simone, Ignacio Corsini, were also on hand to lend their support... The beneficiaries were figures from the world of motor racing,

Olympic athletes, victims of the Luján River floods in Buenos Aires, and even newspaper vendors. When he crossed over to Montevideo to sing at a private party for president Gabriel Terra and on *CX16 Radio Carve*, he made time later to go with his guitarists to the Fermín Ferreyra hospital and perform for the patients there.

This is the best known and documented period of Gardel's life. The direct accounts of it are plentiful, subjective reports that relate what they see as much as what they want to see because Gardel is in fact the image, both artistically and personally, of the desired style to have in the Río de la Plata. He stays out late but returned to the home of his *Vieja*, works like a true professional, has an enormous number of plans for the future, is extroverted and cordial, dresses like a dandy, rises and falls with his art in the different strata of the social pyramid.

Meanwhile, the good business management of his financial affairs by Armando Defino was paying off. He didn't lack for money or work, but he had to prepare for his departure. Hugo Mariani, the orchestra conductor for NBC, the most powerful network of radio stations in the United States, had assured him of the tempting possibility of performing there. The offer appears like a step forward on the route he was looking for. Gardel had remarked on several occasions about his desire and commitment to working in his new profession of movie actor in the North American country. This occasion offered work and connections that were nothing to sneeze it to get a secure foothold in the career he envisioned in his imagination.

His friend Francisco Maschio, owner of the racehorse stalls and racetrack, organized Carlos Gardel's farewell. His most famous friends among artists and people from the turf world were there. Edgardo Donato's Orchestra held nothing back when they played and Gardel sang with his guitarists in this unforgettable party captured in several famous photographs that exist. Razzano was notable by his absence among the people in attendance.

Will (1933)

Before leaving for the United States, Gardel decided to sign a will for an "incalculable inheritance", as Francisco Canaro would describe it later when he was president of the Argentinean Society of Authors and Composers. In it, Gardel declares his mother to be his only heir and appoints Armando Defino as executor. He edited and signed it in anticipation of any fatal incident that could put his mother in dire straits when it came time to dispose of his estate. Straightening out the identity documents from so many years before forced him to do that. He had to clarify his place and date of birth (Toulouse, December 11, 1890), his name before he adopted his artistic one, and his legal status as a single man in an authentic, verifiable way. He did so in order to leave his assets in the hands of the person who had the greatest interest in his life, his mother.

"My true name and surnames are Carlos Romuald Gardes, but due to my profession of artist, I adopted and always used the surname 'Gardel'. I am known everywhere by that name. [...] I do not owe any amount and forgive all those who owe money to me. My assets will be derived from the song titles and papers that may be under my control on the date of my death. [...] I designate as the sole and universal heir of all my assets and rights my named mother, Berthe Gardes".

After that, anyone could and –and will be able to– entertain themselves by fantasizing about his evasions, shortcuts and deflections when that bothersome question about his nationality plagued him:

"I can say I am *rioplatense,* my country is Argentina. An artist, a man of science, has no nationality. Neither does a singer, but since you insist, I'm Uruguayan, born in Tacuarembó. My homeland is the tango. I am a citizen of Corrientes Street".

Many times he had to answer to the chauvinist officer at headquarters, in the band, provincial journalists of an empire that wove together his destiny just as The Fates spin the threads, until one day Atropos decides to use the scissors. They always repeated the same question the police ask a person under arrest: Where are you from? What nationality are you? We have already accounted for his adoption of Tacuarembó as his city of birth as a subterfuge to obtain identity documents that would protect him from potential problems with the French state (the obligation of military enlistment that he never fulfilled).

These complex circumstances merit serious consideration, since for some people being dogmatic about the nationality of tango represents a problem. It was born there on the outskirts of the great *rioplatense* urban centers. It grew bigger and was nourished in other cities in Argentina, including Rosario, Córdoba, Bahía Blanca, etc. The tango also traveled overseas to establish a presence and then grew in Barcelona, Paris, Madrid and other cities. Its global appeal spread the style immediately, setting in motion energies it carries in its root foundation. And it has arrived in the present day with that identity, its status of *rioplatense* origins and growth, reaching people in cities in every continent around the world. These are the characteristics of the tango. It is Finnish, Japanese, Spanish, Italian, Turkish, in short, cosmopolitan. The tango is a popular event, meaning that everyone puts their own soul into it when they experience or perform any of its forms. From its origin and development, it will always be marked as original to Argentina, but it would alter its nature if we conceive of it today as only being of Argentina. Gardel understood it that way and from that came his desire for international projection, the impulse to make it understandable to ears that were unaccustomed to *rioplatense* slang, even as he would never renounce its character as the melody of the suburbs of his beloved Buenos Aires. You can say the tango is now part of the patrimony of humankind; in its records, choreography, ideas about the world and life, in the people who feel it, perform it and dance it.

Este es mi Testamento.

En esta ciudad de Buenos
Aires el día 7 de Noviembre
de 1933, encontrándome en
pleno goce de mis faculta-
des intelectuales otorgo
este mi testamento ológrafo
disponiendo en el de mis bienes
para despues de mi fallecimiento en la siguiente
forma _ primero soy frances
nacido en Toulouse el día
11 de Diciembre de 1890 y soy
hijo de Berthe Gardes.
Segundo. Hago constar expresamente que mi verdadero
nombre y apellido son ___
Carlos Romualdo Gardes
pero con motivo de mi profe-
cion de artista, he adoptado
y usado siempre el apellido
"Gardel" y con este apellido
soy conocido en todas partes.
Asimismo hago constar que los

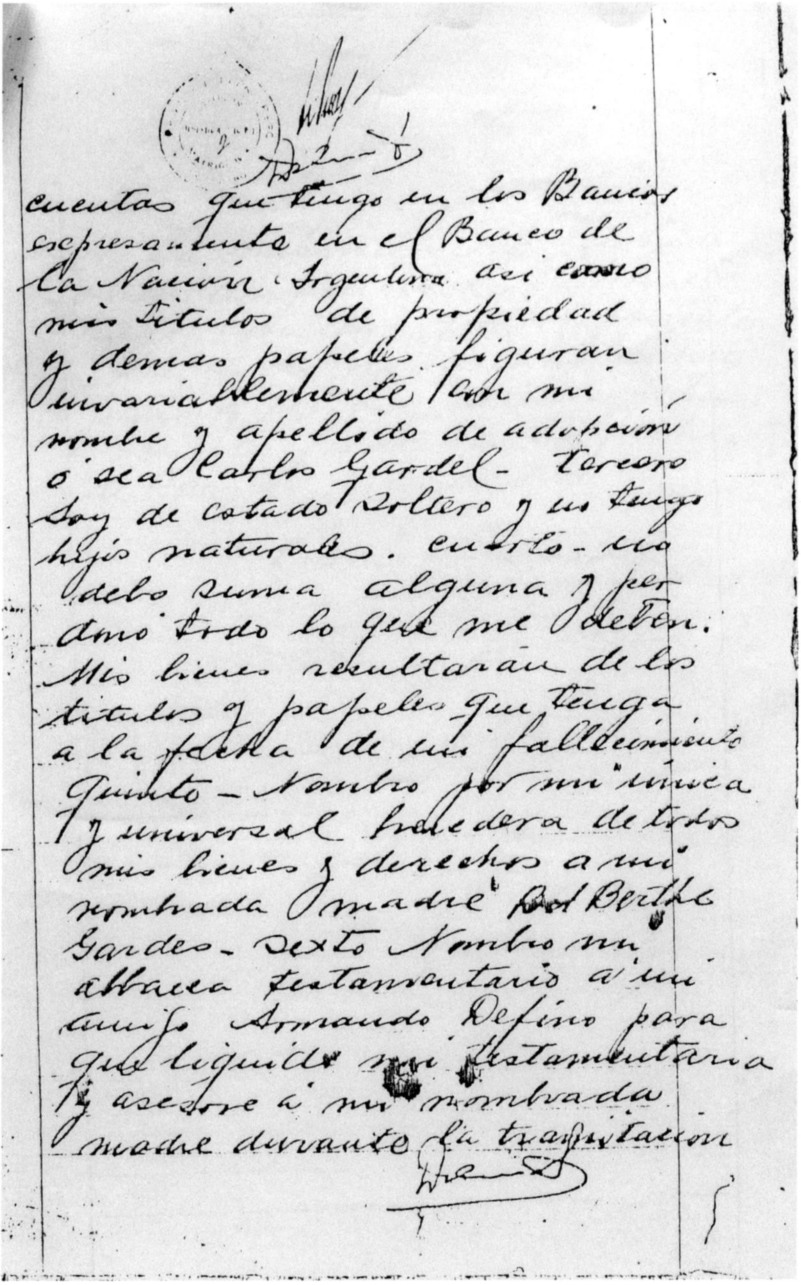

cuentas que tengo en los Bancos
expresamente en el Banco de
la Nación Argentina así como
mis títulos de propiedad
y demás papeles figuran
invariablemente con mi
nombre y apellido de adopción
o sea Carlos Gardel - Tercero
soy de estado soltero y no tengo
hijos naturales. cuarto - no
debo suma alguna y perdono todo lo que me deben.
Mis bienes resultarán de los
títulos y papeles que tenga
a la fecha de mi fallecimiento
Quinto - Nombro por mi única
y universal heredera de todos
mis bienes y derechos a mi
nombrada madre Berthe
Gardes - Sexto Nombro mi
albacea testamentario a mi
amigo Armando Defino para
que liquide mi testamentaria
y asesore a mi nombrada
madre durante la tramitación

Handwritten will of Carlos Gardel.

de la misma — No teniendo
otras disposiciones que hacer
hago constar — que el presente
ha sido redactado de mi
puño y letra y de una sola
vez lo firmo en la fecha
de arriba indicada

Carlos Gardel

REGISTRO NOTARIAL 452 DE LA CAPITAL
HE QUITO
C'BEL
3/67
con su Ori
Buenos Aires 11 de diciembre de 1974

5. EN ROUTE TO THE UNITED STATES (1933)

Gardel embarked on a voyage to the North American nation that held great promise, but first he traveled to France to visit his mother, who was with their family in Toulouse. Later he attended to some business matters and spent a little time with friends and collaborators in Paris. Among the most significant meetings there were with Sally Wakefield, who was now providing capital to invest in his movies, and Alfredo le Pera, who by this point had become his screenwriter and principal poet.

He was accompanied by guitarist Horacio Pettorossi and pianist Alberto Castellano on the ship *Champlain*. They arrived in New York on December 28, 1933 to begin a series of radio performances that were instrumental as the first step in building an impressive artistic presence there in less than two years.

The reception committee included Hugo Mariani, musical director of the NBC radio network and the principal architect behind Gardel's entry into the North American radio world. Violinist and orchestral arranger Terig Tucci, who played a crucial role in creating the musical structures that sprang from Gardel's inspiration, immediately went to work on the arrangements, as he details in his memoirs of that period. They checked into the luxurious Waldorf Astoria hotel and at noon, went to the Ritz

Publicity photo of Gardel at NBC.
He sang for the network the first three months of 1934.

Carlton for an official welcoming lunch for Gardel hosted by the Argentinean Consulate in New York. He soon began the process of adapting to his new environment and started rehearsals for the radio broadcasts accompanied by the network Orchestra. He had never sung with that big an orchestra before and, obviously, the nervousness as they started prompted Gardel's well-remembered instruction to the musicians:

-"You stick to the score, I'm the one who makes the melody."

He sang on NBC Radio and, according to the music director, earned more money than any foreign artist had ever received in the United States. The first tango he sang was *Buenos Aires*, the same one he performed when he said goodbye over the Argentina Radio Nacional network.

David Seitner, the correspondent of the Crítica daily newspaper in Buenos Aires, reported that after his successful debut on NBC, the powerful company who hired Gardel, declared that it was the first time a Latino artist had so completely dominated the ratings among the enormous audience of radio listeners in New York.

"The luxurious rooms at the Waldorf Astoria, where the Argentinean artist was staying, were invaded by a multitude of pretty girls who wanted to get to know the singer personally. And once they witnessed the charismatic charm that radiated from the Latin star up close, their admiration changed into genuine hysteria".

The critic then mentioned the favorable opinions of Gardel's performance expressed by three big North American stars, Eddie Cantor, Al Jolson, and Bing Crosby. Crosby declared:

"Gardel boasts an undeniable musical personality. He has that fourth dimension of singing, knowing how to make his listeners feel what he is singing".

Gardel continued singing on different programs at the radio station during January, February, and March. A trailblazing and original program was transmitted on March 5, when a joint broadcast using radiotelephone technology was set up with the LRY Radio Splendid and LS5 Radio Rivadavia stations in Buenos Aires. The guitarists accompanying his vocals were performing in the latter studio while Gardel used headphones in New York to blend his voice seamlessly with the sound of the guitars over the phone.

Meanwhile, his plans to tour in different Latin American companies, where his European films had already been released, were moving forward even as the arrangements for him to film in New York were gaining momentum. In a letter written to his agent Armando Defino, Gardel was excited over the progress being made and told him:

"We formed a production company named *Éxito's Spanish Pictures* (Hit Spanish Pictures) and I am the director. The company is financed by Western Electric and will be distributed by Paramount".

The married couple of Sally and George Wakefield, the owner of Western Electric, was extremely important in getting the project off the ground, just as they had been in France.

The contract called for filming two movies, with an option for four more. Gardel summoned Le Pera, who was in Paris at the time, and they chose the veteran Louis Gasnier as the director. First, they filmed *Cuesta Abajo*, with a cast of Carlos Gardel, Mona Maris, Vicente Padula, Anita del Campillo, Manuel Peluffo, Carlos Spaventa, Alfredo Le Pera and Jaime Devesa. The team in charge of the music was Alberto Castellano (Pettorossi had returned to Buenos Aires) and Carlos Gardel. Alfredo Le Pera wrote the song lyrics and the screenplay, which features a perennial student, Carlos Acosta, who goes away from his familiar surroundings, leaving a girlfriend behind for an alluring young girl with bewitching eyes. They journey to Paris and New York

New York 1934: Carlos Gardel and his partner Alfredo Lepera

together, barely surviving the problems they encounter along the way as they make their living as tango dancers. The plot development finds the characters going downhill until a friendly ship captain appears who revives the memories of Buenos Aires. Carlos (Acosta) Gardel sings *Mi Buenos Aires Querido* and decides to return to his city. The stellar performance is by actress Mona Maris, with her memorable portrayal of the seductive femme fatale capable of dragging the student away on that adventure.

The filming took place between May 10 and June 1, 1934. Seven songs were featured in the movie, all written by Gardel and Le Pera, and the singer and Mona Maris also dance the tango *Viejos Tiempos*.

New York episodes

Gardel's life in New York contributed a dizzying number of artistic events and projects to his biography. There was a welcome break from worries about money thanks to his radio performances. Gardel wrote in a letter to Defino:

> "I'll send you between 1,000 and 1,500 pesos every month so you can use that to cover expenses. You keep accumulating any money left over and sometimes I'll send you more when things are going good..."

"How am I going to sing words I don't understand, phrases that I don't feel? There is something deep inside me that moves to the sound of the words that are familiar to me and rooted in the most intimate and private parts of my being; words that I learned when I was a child, that mean something about things that are very much our own, and are impossible to translate. My language, gentlemen, is Spanish. Or better still, the Spanish of Argentina, of Buenos Aires".

In fact, things were going better thanks to the filming. Alfredo Le Pera, now his inseparable collaborator, arrived. Gardel had hired Samuel Piza, a native of Costa Rica as an interpreter so that he would help him cope better in the English-speaking country. Similarly, he tried to learn English as fast as he could, first at Mariani's insistence and later on his own initiative. However, when they asked him to sing in that language, he responded with a spirited defense of his mother tongue:

Once Le Pera was there, their energy was directed towards the films. Gardel collaborated on the screenplays prepared by the writer, created the music for the songs, played a part in the auditions of actors and actresses, as well as helping with decisions over the film sets. The rapport between the two men was extraordinary, to the point that the films appear to be varied ways of representing Gardel himself. They crafted scenes in which the leading character was interpreting personality traits originally drawn from Carlos Gardel's real life as part of his role.

Meanwhile, the relationship with Buenos Aires, conducted by exchanging letters and phone calls, was no less moving. Mona Maris commented on that theme in a television interview:

"During the filming of 'Cuesta Abajo', Gardel called his mother on the phone every day and called us over so that we would say hello to her".

He addressed Armando Defino as "my dear brother" and there were many references about the money he should pass along to his guitar boys every month so they could get by financially until he would summon them to accompany him for his recordings and tours. During that period, his recording contract with Odeon passed to RCA Victor. All of his recordings during the final phase of his career were for RCA Victor, and virtually all of them were the songs from his movies.

On the other hand, his relationship with his girlfriend in Buenos Aires was in dire straits. Gardel wrote to Defino:

> "I already told you that it's over as far as I'm concerned, it's over for good and you should look at it that way. I sent a letter telling her that in no uncertain terms and I hope it will be the last one. If they want to keep me as a friend, that's fine. If not, I'll cut her off cold without sending anything more. You should tell her that, and especially her whole family. I'm saying again that I want you to consider this affair is absolutely over and that you spread the word of how I'm thinking to these people. Let's see whether they believe I'm employed by them for my entire life".

Above and beyond the emotional story of the romance, the stance of Isabel Martínez del Valle's family as an interested party is transparently obvious. From various accounts, it is well known that the family harassed the singer with demands for financial assistance from the very earliest stages of the couple's relationship. Although it is possible Gardel's death makes it difficult to imagine that relationship as closed, since Isabel publicly honored his memory by proclaiming their love and sharing the mourning and devotions with his mother Berta Gardes.

Gardel had moved from the Waldorf Astoria hotel in New York to an elegant apartment in the Beaux Arts building that he shared with pianist Alberto Castellano and Alfredo Le Pera. Their life in the city was stimulated by long walks and reconnaissance missions to take in its cosmopolitan character as well as the work they shared. They explored the stores and well-known sites, kept on top of the latest developments in movies and musical shows

Carlos Gardel signs his contract with Paramount Pictures.
Although Gardel was nominally independent, Paramount
Pictures was behind the four films he made in New York.
Photo courtesy Arturo Yepez.

around town, and ate in down-to-earth Italian family restaurants.
Le Pera didn't always go along when they went out, since he was
"furiously" occupied in writing the screenplays for the next
movies. It must be mentioned that the brilliance of his star shined
brightest during those four years when he was Gardel's artistic
partner. He argued with Castellano, with the directors and actors of
the films, and was blessed with a "very quick sense of humor,
albeit a little oblique", as Terig Tucci recalls in his memoirs. When
he was visited by an Italian nobleman on one occasion, Le Pera
was so absorbed in his writing that he forgot all about him. After
waiting around indefinitely, the irritated man introduced himself
again:

> "Please be aware that you are in the presence of Pedro Juan
> Ramón de los Llanos, Count of Sicily and Ladrón de Guevara".

To which Le Pera replied, without lifting his eyes from the paper:

"Well, pull up half-a-dozen chairs and sit yourself down..."

If one looks closely at the texts of Le Pera's songs, you can sense the overwhelming and somewhat tormented inner life he was experiencing in those years. When he appeared on the scene, the tango already had its mythology in place. However, this writer gave a special treatment to its most common settings: the neighborhood, the streetlight, small dance halls, streets, the good times and nostalgic memories... a new approach to the faraway and longing. Le Pera's pen also renews the wandering main characters of the tango who blend together in a true literary bohemia, engaging in existential searches that render futile every impulse to become eternal anywhere in the world or in life. We pass through life and in passing we are subject to love, hate, hope, grief, solitude and wonderful company. It is in the awareness of this range of emotions around us when the flow of time becomes clearer to us. There is, in short, a constant effort of feeling nostalgia for faraway lands that are consumed and checked by lost loves but are persistent in evoking them.

Despite that, Le Pera's style adapted well to the nature of the musical comedies he was preparing for the second Gardel movie filmed in the United States, *El Tango on Broadway*.

Musical comedy and the premiere of Cuesta Abajo (1934)

In a letter dated April 23, 1934, Gardel gave his friend and agent Defino advance notice that he would film *Cuesta Abajo*, an "American-style musical comedy with plenty of girls and maybe some good revue scenes". The plot tells of the adventures of a

"Cuesta Abajo", the first film he made in New York,
had its premiere at a theater in Spanish Harlem in Manhattan.
Gardel made a personal appearance there to mark the big day.

cajetilla from Buenos Aires now well versed in tangos and spending his money in New York. The ambiance of parties, young women and music changes when his uncle arrives from Argentina to oversee the dissolute life of the young man. But in the end the latter manages to drag his uncle along into the New York nightlife, conquered by the *rioplatense* tangos. Gardel played the role of the young man, the film's lead character. He sang the *zamba Caminito Soleado*, two beautiful tangos, *Soledad* and *Golondrinas,* and a foxtrot, *Rubias en Nueva York.* The last was inspired musically even though the lyrics were inferior to all of Le Pera's other songs. Agustín Cornejo, an Argentinean folk artist living in New York, sings two *criollo* songs he wrote himself: the *zamba "Chinita"* and the *cifra "Qué Me Importa"?*

Everyone was satisfied with the way the film turned out. However, the arguments between screenwriter Le Pera and director Louis Gasnier were so vehement that Paramount decided to replace the latter. His place was taken by John Reinhardt, also well-remembered for a phrase worth pondering concerning Gardel's voice: "The man sings with a tear in his throat".

The new director smoothed over some, but not all, of the difficulties. It was very complicated to reproduce the authentic *criollo* environments, as La Pera and Gardel desired, in the context of the assembly line productions that Paramount expected. The issue of their ongoing demand for Latin American and Spanish actors became an obsession that was never resolved. Gardel even entertained the notion of possibly filming again in Joinville, where they could find the cast of skilled actors these films required due to its proximity to Spain. On the other hand, it is worth bearing in mind that the "roadmap for filmmaking" in those days didn't exist much beyond its basic outlines. The people involved in making films knew, especially Gardel, that they had to improve by learning from experience and improved production conditions. The journalist Rodríguez Peña stated in *La Nación* daily newspaper in 1966 that Gardel told him during a conversation:

"The plots of those first films are not good enough and I was too quick to make excuses for them. They served our purpose of making movies with genuine enthusiasm and popular flavor. Other phases will come soon..."

The Medellín tragedy leaves us with this big question mark, although observing his improvement as a composer and actor over the course of his brief film career, it could be expected that the future would bring some particularly interesting new developments, just as he anticipated.

As opposed to some opinions expressed by others, like the writer Julio Cortázar, I believe that there were "neither renunciations nor betrayals" during this stage on the part of Gardel. On the contrary, his attitude was just the opposite, reflected in his search for Latin American and Spanish songs and actors to be featured performers in his movies. Even more, as we noted before, at some point he thought of going back from the United States to France due to its proximity to Spain and the Spanish-speaking world.

After filming the second movie in the United States, *Tango on Broadway*, his intention was to return to France, where his mother had traveled after his absence from Buenos Aires. However, that trip was delayed by various circumstances, which enabled him to make more recordings and travel around the city, this time accompanied by Astor Piazzolla, then just a kid who lived in New York. He also attended the North American premiere of his film *Cuesta Abajo* on August 10, 1934 at the Teatro Campoamor on the corner of 5th Avenue and 116th Street in New York. It was preceded by an announcement of the surprise appearance of Carlos Gardel "in person" via distribution of a letter from the singer promising that he would be "pleased" to attend. Journalist Mary M. Spaulding of the Cuban magazine *Carteles* wrote of the premiere:

Carlos Gardel and the "blondes from New York".
They appeared in the second film he made in New York,
"El Tango en Broadway"

"There were two blocks packed with people who waited, battled and maneuvered their way through the crowd for the chance to buy a ticket. When Gardel appeared on a balcony, illuminated by the spotlights, the audience gave him a standing ovation. It was a tremendous ovation by everyone there that made the theater shake".

The musician Terig Tucci insists in his book *Gardel in New York:*

"After the show was sold out, there were still thousands of people pressing up against the theater door, struggling to get in and spilling out onto the sidewalk and street so much that they made it impossible for pedestrians or cars to circulate. The company had to place loudspeakers in the street in deference to those people who could not get in the theater".

Obviously, the number of Latin American moviegoers in the United States was quite large and Carlos Gardel had become a star for them that they took as their own, a reflection of their own dreams.

During that period, he recorded eight songs with an Orchestra conducted by Tucci and two more backed by guitars and pianist Alberto Castellano. On August 17, 1934 there was a new NBC broadcast in conjunction with *Radio Splendid* of Buenos Aires which was transmitted in Brazil, Uruguay and Canada. Gardel sang three songs from his recent movies in New York with the orchestra of Hugo Mariani. For the finale, he performed three more tangos accompanied by his guitarists in Buenos Aires. A few statements about this episode from the man who was now the indisputable King of Tango bear considering:

"I'm not the one who's successful. It's our tango that is so admired".

On August 25, he embarked for Europe and remained there for a month and a half before returning to the United States where the activity was once again at a fever pitch. A vibrant daily life was waiting that he would experience after moving into an apartment at the Middletown Hotel in New York. His collaborator Le Pera rented another one next to Gardel's. In a long letter to Defino, he spoke about a wide-ranging assortment of his concerns, perspectives, and projects. He evaluated the results of the last two films in the letter and tacitly acknowledged how much they must improve in executing these film projects. He distanced himself from his ex-partner Razzano once and for all. He knew through his friend Osvaldo Fresedo that Razzano "is indignant about the abuse of the tango *Cuesta Abajo* that they play on the radio 20 times every day". He gave some tips on acquiring scripts and artists to join him in the company to improve his movie career. He directed Defino to tell his collaborator Alberto Castellano, who was then in Buenos Aires:

"...to get ready to travel to the United States and have melodies with him to give brilliant musical accompaniment for the films. As for tangos, he should bring those only if it's something phenomenal. If not, I prefer to do them myself".

Then he recommended that Defino talk to the guitarists about the still-postponed tour they would do through various Latin American countries. That tour ended, as is well-known, in the tragedy of Medellín.

In that same letter, he writes about Isabel Martínez del Valle, asking Defino to let her know:

"She shouldn't have any illusions or high hopes about me. Everything you know about is still in effect. The monthly subsidies are finished, and you should not give them one cent more under any circumstances. Concerning the house, we will go on paying for it gradually without it being a burden on us, in order not to lose what we already paid and to return courtesy for the shameless things they did. You know what my dreams are for the future: I want to work for myself, to give a good life to my mother and be able to enjoy 30 years of work with four old friends".

Later in the letter he recapitulates his recent days in France. The family reunions of Berta Gardes, who had to pack her bags one day in 1892 and emigrate with her son who was not even three years old, affected Gardel. It is striking to see the level of interest shown by close and distant relatives who met to get to know this young man who was building such a brilliant career.

"I have a plan to buy a house in Nice, for my mother and us. The weather is ideal for her and I will find one with all the comforts of home for everyone. The houses are cheap there. This is a project, but we are already studying it. I had some great times with my mother, who is fine. And I got to know a family that I never thought I would have, all really good people and very pleasant to be around".

His continuing passion for the "donkeys" is evident right to the very end of this letter. He sends greetings to his friends Maschio and Leguisamo:

> "Be patient with the horses, let's hope the donkeys improve. If we don't buy any this year, we'll buy some next year".

New York, second phase (1935)

Numerous people, artistic partners and friends who were with Gardel in the final period of his life left their accounts and reflections on the man. It is certainly true that the untimely, premature death in the airplane accident prompted this abundance of recollections. Among them are biographical sketches that not only comment on the facts of Gardel's life but are also expressions of affection or rejection on the part of each individual writer.

Memories of Gardel's fondness for jokes, sometimes risque ones, are frequent. He would probably be letting off steam by telling jokes that amused him and helped clear his mind from the understandable pressure created by his unfailing dedication and responsibility towards his work. At the same time, it was a tactic he adopted to become one of the guys and more familiar to the artists who surrounded him in new situations. When he was finalizing the possibility of filming *Tango Bar*, he sent a telegram calling on actor Tito Lusiardo:

> "Travel right away. I need you within 15 days. Ask Delia to forgive me. Budget prevents bringing her. Regards, Carlos".

When Lusiardo arrived in New York, a taxi took him to the hotel where the singer was waiting for him. The cab driver left his bag of clothes on the sidewalk. Gardel had assured him that he could leave the bag there and go inside to check into his room because "in this country, no one touches anything that isn't theirs". But when he came back out, Lusiardo couldn't find a trace of his luggage. When the hotel employees had no information, he had to admit to his dismay that his belongings had been stolen. Imagine his surprise when he woke up the next day and found the bag alongside his bed. Gardel had played a joke on him by hiding it in the hotel basement.

"And, old man, you had to pay the room rate!"

In December 1934, Paramount shot a PR film *Cazadores de Estrellas* spotlighting the great artists who were lighting up their sound movie screens. Bing Crosby, Ethel Merman, and Ray Noble and his band were some of the artists featured. It also included Carlos Gardel, whose fame was extending beyond the widespread boundaries of the Spanish-language movie market. He sang two representative pieces, *Apure Delantero Buey*, a song; and *Amargura,* a tango. Manuel Peluffo, Carlos Spaventa and Celia Villa framed his performance by staging a brief romantic story in two sketches. When they filmed the scene with a passionate kiss, Gardel made a deal with the director for Spaventa and Villa to continue kissing each other after the definitive take, under the pretext that the "the scene must be more convincing". The cameras continued to pretend they were rolling normally until the couple discovered the joke when Gardel cracked up laughing after the fifth take.

In the give-and-take discussions with Le Pera concerning the arguments and characters he should portray and embody, Gardel demanded them to be so custom-made for him that Le Pera's scathing comeback was:

"You don't need a writer. What you need is a tailor".

Since he returned from his European trip on October 15, 1934,

Carlos Gardel, Alfredo Lepera, and argentine actor Tito Lusiardo
play in the snow outside Astoria Studios in New York.
All of Gardel's New York films were made at Astoria.
Photo courtesy Héctor Rebasti

he immersed himself in adapting contracts for the new films,
reviewing and revising Le Pera's screenplays, and having the two
of them go over the texts he was having sent from Buenos Aires. In
his capacity as the main character and co-producer of the films, he
chose actors and the orchestrations for the music he composed
almost in its entirety. He called his guitarists for the planned tour of
Central and South American countries. When they reached New
York, Barbieri, Riverol and Aguilar were detained for a long time
at customs, as the North American immigration laws had
prohibited the entry of any workers, musicians included. Gardel
had to post a bond so that they were allowed to disembark,
pretending to fire them in a fit of fake anger:

"But what kind of bullshit did you do so that they made you prisoners?"

The filming of *El Día que Me Quieras*, directed by John Reinhardt for Paramount, began on January 14, 1935. Gardel told Defino in a letter:

"The movie should have taken 13 days but the filming lasted for 18, and more work than usual was required in every sense. But I'm very happy with the results and I think the film we just finished is much superior to everything I've done until now".

The pace of activity started to accelerate again. He immediately announced the start of the next film shoot for February 18 and now had some very experienced and well-known actors to count on. However, his determination to do things as well as he possibly could occupied all his waking hours and days. The next and final movie was *Tango Bar*, also directed by Reinhardt. It was a musical comedy that intertwined love stories, horse races out at the track, a transatlantic ocean liner with immigrants and a bar in Barcelona where part of the movie takes place. Gardel again dances a tango, *Tiempos Viejos*, this time with Rosita Moreno, and shines in performing some of the memorable pieces he wrote: the tangos *Por una Cabeza* and *Arrabal Amargo* and *Lejana Tierra Mía*, a song with a touch of pasodoble at the start. The music to *Por una Cabeza* was whipped up by the singer during a sleepless night spent searching for the appropriate melody to use on top of the literary base provided by Alfredo Le Pera. Terig Tucci wrote in his memoirs that Gardel didn't know formal musical notation so he invented a system for the piano using bits of paper placed on each key, indicating what the notes were by a letter and how long they should last with numbers. That was the way Gardel composed, generally at night, when fragments of some melodies to his famous tangos would come that Terig transferred to musical staff paper the

Carlos Gardel and Rosita Moreno in "El Dia que me Quieras".
This film was turned out to be his biggest box office success.

next day. Tucci also relates in his book *Gardel in New York:*

- "The phone rings at three in the morning. Half asleep, I picked up the phone and hear Gardel's voice. He tells me with obvious satisfaction:

- 'Che, Viejo, I just found a cool melody for the tango *Por una Cabeza'* and proceeded to sing it for me right away. I don't know if it was because I still wasn't completely awake but hearing the fruits of his inspiration over the phone, neither the melody or lyrics made much of an impression on me and I told him that. Somewhat pissed off, Gardel answered me with his trademark sarcasm:

- 'Listen, Beethoven, you stay with your eighth notes and sixty-fourth notes, but don't mess with me when it's a question of horses'".

Gardel is the center of attention during filming of "Tango Bar",
his last film.

During the 1990s, two famous Hollywood movies used that
inspiration of Gardel to provide the ambiance for key moments in
their plots: *Por una Cabeza* is featured in a dance in "Schindler's
List" by Steven Spielberg and Martin Brest's "Scent of a Woman",
when Al Pacino and Gabrielle Anwar pair up.

Investigations conducted by tenacious biographers delving
deep into Gardel's life have contributed significant revelations
about his relationship with Paramount. In fact, the Great
Depression of 1929 left its disastrous mark on the giant movie
company. At the end of 1931, the decision was made to consider
closing its studios in Bombay, Paris, and New York. The only
Spanish-language films they continued doing in France were the
ones starring Gardel and a few with Imperio Argentina. They were
box office hits, *Las Luces de Buenos Aires* first and later *Melodía
de Arrabal.*

According to the observations of César Fratantoni, by 1934 the Depression had halted most filming at the Astoria Studios in New York but thanks to its central location and Paramount's heavy investments before the crisis, Astoria Studios had some of the best film equipment in the world. Gardel's films could count on using that state-of-the-art material for the era. It should be noted that the films were done because it was highly profitable to invest in the Argentinean artist and the world he represented. The main scenes of the screenplays were filmed with him and they had plans to continue that were ruined by the accident in Medellin. According to Arturo Yépez-Pottier, Paramount was interested in "the possibility that the actor would turn into the next Valentino", and in the end "the gaucho would make millions for the company."

With all his film shoots finished, Gardel went into the radio stadios to do a broadcast from the United States to Argentina for LR3 *Radio Belgrano.* Accompanied by Hugo Mariani's Orchestra, he sang *Soledad, Golondrinas, Rubias de Nueva York* and *Caminito Soleado.*

His last recording sessions took place on March 19 and 20 at RCA Victor studios. An Orchestra conducted by Terig Tucci accompanied him on ten songs and the guitars of Barbieri, Riverol, and Aguilar on one. His last recording was on March 25, consisting of nothing more than the words to an advertisement and greeting from the RCA Victor label.

The Caribbean tour

Gardel finally embarked for the Caribbean countries with a sizable entourage that included guitarists, assistants, and businessmen. Alfredo Le Pera, his secretary and sound technician José Corpas Moreno and his English teacher José Plaja went with him on the voyage that lasted from March 28 -- April 1, 1935. Professional orchestras of maracas players were on board during the journey of the packet (mail) boat *Coamo,* cheering up the days

Gardel meets the press on his arrival in Puerto Rico.
Photo courtesy Arturo Yepez.

of the carefree travelers. According to J. M. Aguilar, Carlos Gardel danced the son, the hip rhythm that was en vogue at the time. Their first stop was Puerto Rico, where a large crowd was waiting for them, including journalists from the major media outlets, Paramount representatives, and the governor of the island. In fact, the goal of the film company was to take advantage of the tour to promote the movies filmed at their studios. For that reason, many of the places where Gardel performed in the countries he visited were theaters affiliated with Paramount. The daily newspaper *El Mundo* reported that close to three thousand people were unable to get into the theater for his debut performance in Puerto Rico. When Gardel found out, defying the producers, he opened the windows of a dressing room facing the street and sang three tangos for the crowd outside. The first one was *Caminito*. Later, he demanded that the production company lower ticket prices "even though it may be detrimental to my own earnings".

His Puerto Rico stay included a visit with the governor. From April 3 till 22, he performed in concert halls in fourteen different towns. In every case, the sheer number of his followers spilled over onto the adjacent sidewalks and streets. On the day he departed, April 23, thousands of Puerto Ricans went to the dock to see Gardel off as he boarded a boat bound for Venezuela.

It arrived at La Guayra, where another sizable crowd was waiting and made it difficult for him to reach the Miramar hotel. He traveled to Caracas by train on another day. But the heat there was too hard to take, a problem that would surface constantly throughout the tour. Just like what happened in La Guayra, there was a huge crowd waiting when they reached the station that far exceeded and overwhelmed an inept, surprised police detail there. The police responded with force, causing injuries to several people, among them Alfredo Le Pera, who they had mistaken for just another admirer.

Gardel debuted at the Teatro Principal in Caracas. After ten days of performances there, he moved on to Valencia and Maracay, and later to Maracaibo and Cabimas, two areas enjoying great prosperity thanks to the booming oil industry.

In the Caribbean, Gardel experienced the devotion of an audience that was the cumulative result of a body of work and fame that now knew no frontiers. He had never seen that level of enthusiasm in Argentina, although Defino was telling him in his letters:

> "The results of the premiere of *Cuesta Abajo* in Buenos Aires are fantastic. They had to stop the screening several times so they could do encores of your songs".

There are enough accounts to suggest that Gardel felt pressed by the tour schedule which was going on longer than expected because it was so successful. He received good news from

Paramount about getting bigger budgets for his films due to the substantial profits earned by the earlier ones. Maybe he would have been able to film a movie on the poet Evaristo Carriego, an idea that was already sketched out in Le Pera's imagination, as a great musical about the tango. The writer accompanied Gardel for the whole tour, crafting screenplays and songs. He wasn't satisfied with the work they had already done, you had to progress and move forward. In a letter to Defino dated March 24, 1935, Le Pera wrote:

> "It would be misleading to tell you everything was unsuccessful due to a series of obstacles that conspired to place us in a situation of overwhelming inertia and complete demoralization. *El Día que Me Quieras* is, or was, the finest film we made... well, after the script was approved by Paramount, the same old stuff started up again, the battles with the director, who doesn't understand and falsifies the scenes, dehumanizing them or turning them into circuses. By fighting diligently, we managed to achieve an interesting cohesion and unity to the film despite the director. Then came the inevitable: the massacre of the editing. And the true *criollo* films die there".

The idea of returning to Argentina to make films, in an industry that was beginning to show promising results, was probably on his mind. This new horizon was becoming a kind of obsession. Movies had been responsible in large part for Gardel's rising popularity, who was still taking an active interest in the local rhythms over the course of the tour. He learned to dance the *joropo* in Venezuela and recommended to his guitarists that they should be picking up on the discoveries from the hotbed of musical creativity that was the Caribbean. *Pasillos, bambucos, guabillas,* etc., were styles that he received advance notice of through Terig Tucci, who had lived in Colombia for several years before settling in New York.

Gardel's appearances accompanied the premieres of his latest movies. He sang the recent tangos from his films along with classics like *Caminito, Mano a Mano, El Carretero, Tengo Miedo,*

Insomnio, etc. He was an artist who identified with expressions and displays of popular joy, knew how to appreciate it and take it to an even higher level.

From Venezuela he moved on to Curaçao, the Dutch island in the Lesser Antilles. The inhabitants spoke Papiamento, a local language that blends Spanish, English, and Dutch. He encountered an enthusiastic audience there, too, who called Gardel "master". After that, they arrived on the island of Aruba for a single performance and returned by plane to Curaçao. It was Gardel's first trip using that form of transportation. On June 4, he wrote to Defino:

> "Both Curaçao and Aruba are Dutch colonies. Aruba is an oil industry island, but all the inhabitants know me and love me. They call me 'master'".

They arrived at the city of Barranquilla, Colombia, the final country in the life of Carlos Gardel. After the brief rest, he continued their trip to gorgeous Cartagena, where a packed house thrilled to his art. He should have declined the offers of new, unscheduled performances that were being added to the itinerary, as much for the intense heat there as his desire to recapture his old pace of filmmaking. His entourage was further swelled by local businessmen who were basking in the reflected glory of traveling with the King of Tango.

He flew to Medellín to perform on June 11-13, as well as greeting the audience of local radio station *Ecos de la Montaña* (Echoes of the Mountain). He went to the capital, Bogotá, from Medellín. He was preceded by Le Pera, Plaza, and Paramount executive Henry Swartz in order to finalize the details of his appearance in that city. Ten thousand people had gathered at Techo Airport to greet Gardel's arrival, an unprecedented crowd. He was traveling on SCADTA, one of the two Colombian airline companies and financed by German capital. The SACO company was owned by a Colombian-North American corporation. The airplane had to take special evasive maneuvers to avoid crashing into the public who had invaded the landing strip. In keeping with his customary sense of humor, Gardel wrote to Defino:

> "The reception in Bogotá was incredible. When the plane approached, the people rushed towards it. The pilot had to turn halfway around and head to another landing strip so that a tragedy wouldn't occur. But a tragedy happened anyway. They robbed this worthless fool I have working for me of his wallet with some 'mangos' that belonged to me. At least it wasn't that much and Colombian".

The "worthless fool" was his secretary Azzaf, and the "mangos" his money.

Getting from the airport to the hotel turned out to be quite complicated because there were so many people on the highway. That same night, June 14, Gardel sang in the Teatro Real of Bogota and continued there through June 17, causing a genuine popular uproar. He sang at the *Teatro Olympia* from June 18-21 and returned to the Teatro Real for his final performances on June 22-23. But his final appearance took place after the event in the studios of radio station *La Voz de la Victor*, his record company at the time. The session was specially prepared for his farewell from Colombia. Loudspeakers were placed in the Plaza Bolívar that the radio studios faced. Both the plaza and the adjacent streets were packed with people who listened to Gardel singing *Cuesta Abajo, Tengo Miedo, Insomnio, Melodía de Arrabal, No Te Engañes*, and *Corazón*. Later he spoke into the microphones:

> "I'm leaving Bogota with the impression that I am staying in your hearts... I feel in the gaze of the Colombian women, the smile of the children who remind me so much of the children in my own country, and the applause of the Bogota audiences, a warm affection towards me. If somebody somewhere asks me sometime about the best receptions I've received throughout my career, I assure you that I won't be able to keep from mentioning the Colombian people.

June 24 1935: Gardel reads a tourist guide before boarding
he airplane that will, later that day,
be involved in the accident that caused his death.

Thank you, my friends...thank you very much for all your kindness.
I'm going to see my mother soon and I don't know if I'll be back,
because man proposes, but God disposes. But the charm of this
country that welcomed me and now is saying farewell as if I was one
of its own is so great that I can't say goodbye to you... just until we
meet again... until we meet again, my friends".

After those words, he concluded the session by singing the
tango *Silencio*. Then he went to the windows that allowed him to
hear the roars of approval from the 5,000 people who had
surrounded *La Voz de la Victor* and sang *Tomo y Obligo* from there.

One way trip, June 24,1935

At noon on June 24, the group again found itself at Techo Airport to begin their trip to the city of Cali, where Gardel was scheduled for his last performance in Colombia. There were drinks, embraces and photographs as they said goodbye. The airplane took off with Gardel and his entourage on board. It had to make a technical stopover at the Olaya Herrera Airport in Medellin, to refuel and change pilots. A crowd was waiting for them again. Several schools had suspended their afternoon classes to greet the artist. After a snack, the passengers returned to the airplane piloted by Colombian native Ernesto Samper Mendoza, the owner and pilot of SACO, assisted by 18-year-old Willis Foster. With everyone seated, the F31 of the SACO company began to taxi to gain speed for take-off. Another F31 of the SCADTA company named *Manizales* was waiting at the other end of the runway to take off after the plane carrying Gardel and his party.

According to several reports, there existed an acute rivalry between the two companies, who were battling for supremacy in the Colombian skies. On June 20, SCADTA shareholder and pilot Ulrich Thom had flown a mere five meters above Samper Mendoza's airplane. He was a man with great self-esteem, a kind of hero in the Colombian aviation world. Gardel had made the flight from Medellin to Bogota with SCADTA, and the prestige of the airlines was also enhanced by the "social weight" of the passengers that flew with them.

The events that ended that take-off sequence was a horrifying collision of the two airplanes and subsequent burning of both planes. It ended the lives of the seven passengers on the *Manizales* when the SACO F31 crashed into it. Eight of the 13 passengers riding on the latter plane died at the scene: Carlos Gardel, Alfredo Le Pera, Guillermo Barbieri, José Corpas Moreno, Celedonio Palacios, Henry Swartz, Willis Foster and Samper Mendoza himself. Four were saved with horrible burns. Ángel D. Riverol and Alfonso Azzaf succumbed to their injuries within hours, while José María Aguilar and José Plaja lived on for years bearing the permanent scars from that tragedy. Grant Flynt, the air traffic director, only suffered some bruises, thanks to the fact he was standing at the side of the cabin door and fell to the ground before flames from the exploding fuel tanks engulfed him.

No definitive explanation emerged that conclusively put an end to the rampant speculation about the accident. One theory spoke of a gust of wind that knocked Gardel's plane off course while another mentioned a dispute between passengers and the pilot. A third version puts the blame on a mechanical failure that Samper Mendoza could not control. There has even been speculation about a shot fired from the *Manizales*. It is true that the best witness, Grant Flynt, who only suffered minor injuries, was never seen or heard from again after the accident. In our opinion, the rivalry between the two companies is the most plausible version, given that the feared response to Ulrich Thom's earlier provocation was in Samper Mendoza's hands. Shortly after the plane he was piloting began to move forward, it took an inexplicable "turn to the right in a curve 80 meters long until it was 30 degrees off the axis of the runway, leaving it for the taxiing lane towards the right in the direction of the *Manizales*. The latter plane had its engines running, ready to begin the take-off sequence. It seems likely that Samper would have tried making a risky pass over the *Manizales* to pay the German pilot back for his earlier audacious stunt, and he lost control of his plane during the attempt. If that is the way it happened, the fact that no official organization would be willing to officially admit that these actions of individual recklessness escaped them is of serious concern, with their fatal consequences for all the precautions.

This year, 2019, bookstores just received a work compiled by Mauricio and Manuela Umana that finally brought to print a book written by the lawyer Alfonso Uribe Misas, the attorney for SCADTA in the trial against SACO based on the accident in Medellin. The author was going to publish that book in 1938 but it was banned by the then-president of Colombia, Alfonso López Pumarejo, since "he considered it a problem for the government". It contains fundamental, documented revelations that support the suspicions and notes we collected and expressed in the first edition of this book, in 2003. What are they, briefly summarized?

a) Samper Mendoza had a pilot license that did not allow him to fly with passengers. No way was he licensed to fly a F31, a trimotor for commercial flights. But because he was a member of a powerful, monied, well-connected family, the Colombian government ignored its own laws and regulations and granted Samper a flight license after he bought two F31s in the United States. The co-pilot at the time of the accident was Willis Foster, a young 18-year-old kid, a general mechanic's apprentice with no flight experience.

b) According to several witness accounts, the load of the 13 passengers on the SACO F31 exceeded the limit by 600 pounds, since Gardel insisted on bringing all his luggage and equipment on the plane. It was already overweight when it flew from Bogota to Medellin and they added even more heavy trunks and the flammable negatives of his movies there.

c) On the runway, the SACO plane that Samper Mendoza piloted, began its take-off run with severe tailwinds, an unacceptable and unauthorized practice in aviation. The plane moved northward, when suddenly, the plane swerved to the right side, heading straight into the "Manizales" SCADTA plane. The outcome was that without having reached full take-off from the ground the SACO plane collided head on with the SCADTA plane, which was waiting for its turn to reach the threshold for take off.

In their statements to the press and court in Colombia, the survivors J. M. Aguilar and José Plaja, agreed on their astonishment over the abrupt swerve of Samper Mendoza's F31 towards the place where the other plane was sitting. Plaja explains: "... I thought Samper wanted to fly over the place where the Manizales was." After all the investigations conducted, inspections, studies and reports from experts, the court surprisingly and, at the very least questionably, concluded that "...anyone who could be held criminally responsible for what happened died in the airplane crash, ruling that no one would be charged and brought to criminal trial."

In short, the book by Uribe Misas *La Verdad Sobre la Muerte de Carlos Gardel* (The Truth About the Death of Carlos Gardel) explains and clarifies the background, processes and results of a tangled trial that lasted three years. We've read so many newspaper headlines over the years that pointedly declare *Gardel killed himself* that we're sick of them. In light of the new facts presented, it's not inappropriate to bluntly turn the assertion around in the question "Was he killed?" Or did death simply fall upon him and we will always reject that the ending to his life was so senseless, so gratuitous, so much by chance? The Greeks say that all excess is an act of hubris, and neither the gods nor the sea escape the punishment of committing hubris. The obvious excesses of Samper Mendoza spread its punishment out among 15 people, all unrelated to him and absolutely innocent. And one of them, the singer Carlos Gardel, was tragically cut down in the prime of his stellar life.

Armando Defino and his wife Adela traveled to Colombia to recover the bodies of Carlos Gardel and his companions. He also had to settle the pending money matters and recover the belongings of the singer. They had to transfer the funeral remains to Panama in a long, roundabout journey that ended up in New York. The remains were then taken to Buenos Aires aboard the ship *Pan American*, arriving there months later on February 5, 1936. Before reaching their final destination, they made a stop in Montevideo, where an anguished crowd remained permanently on the customs dock to keep watch over the body. Once back in Buenos Aires, his mother Berta was joined by tens of thousands of people who accompanied the remains of the singer with tango music and songs following the public viewing in Luna Park. He

1936: Gardel's funeral in Buenos Aires.

was laid to rest in a simple but dignified mausoleum at La Chacarita cemetery.

The Gardel Mausoleum in the Chacarita Cemetery,
Buenos Aires. Built in 1937, it is still the most visited place
in the cemetery.

EPILOGUE

Day after day, people from all around the world approach his tomb to pay homage with mementos and offerings, the ultimate gesture in the sincere ceremony of listening to Carlos Gardel singing his never-ending tango.

Is Gardel a legend? He has been granted the stele of the larger-than-life individual and it has projected him towards a place where it is necessary for us to complete the house of life, so well-furnished today with perishable things and ephemeral lights. However, the power and strength of his artistic achievements are so intense that we prefer the pleasure of hearing them time and time again over any rituals of worship venerating him.

He died young and at the peak of his career. We didn't see him decline over time. Like the classic hero, he stayed triumphant against any difficulties and dangers lurking in wait. Generous enough in his everyday behavior, he lavished his singing on us not only by searching for a better form but presenting us with the gift of producing more songs than could reasonably be expected of a recording career using the limited technical media of that era. He went above and beyond himself, according to what the contemporary collective imagination desires, rising up from the bottom where most of the human race exists. It is painful to us that he went away at 44 years old, being a modern young man shaped by the changing codes of our cities. He is there with his voice and image, his legacy perpetuated in the anecdotes that are always coming forward, facing his destiny with an undeniable joie de vivre. For that reason, we are very far away from those who maintain: "He was lucky enough to die burned", an opinion repeated by Ernesto Sábato on Spanish television in 1992. Gardel experienced the horrible misfortune of dying in that tragedy... some people took advantage of that to pose theories, among others the one that his coronation and consecration as a legend was based on the final fatal fire. The documents in plain view are eloquent: During his lifetime, Carlos Gardel was the Greatest, the Complete Singer, the Master, the Thrush among the *criollo* singers, the King of Tango.

We lament his death, but in no way would that justify our complaints over what he would have been able to accomplish. It is all there in the immense work whose magnitude we have tried to sketch out her. Would there be that much more in the work of Rimbaud, Poe, Mozart, Vallejo... if they had the additional years of life they missed out on? No one can affirm what they would have added with any certainty. Meanwhile, we feel their giant steps making the earth resonate.

SECOND PART

FILMOGRAPHY

'FLOR DE DURAZNO'   1917
Produced by: Patria Film.
Directed by: Francisco Defilipis Novoa.
Starring: Carlos Gardel, Ilda Pirovano, Diego Figueroa and Celestino Petray.

'ENCUADRE DE CANCIONES'   1930
Produced by: Movietone.
Directed by: Eduardo Morera.
Starring: Carlos Gardel, Celedonio Flores, Enrique S. Discépolo, Arturo de Nava and Francisco Canaro.

'LUCES DE BUENOS AIRES'   1931
Produced by: Paramount.
Directed by: Adelqui Millar.
Starring: Carlos Gardel, Sofía Bozán, Gloria Guzmán and Vicente Padula.

'ESPÉRAME'   1932

Produced by: Paramount.
Directed by: Louis Gasnier.
Starring: Carlos Gardel, Goyita Herrero, Lolita Benavente
               and Jaime Devesa.

'LA CASA ES SERIA'   1932

Produced by: Paramount.
Directed by: Louis Gasnier.
Starring: Carlos Gardel, Imperio Argentina, Lolita
               Benavente and Josita Hernán.

'MELODÍA DE ARRABAL'   1932

Produced by: Paramount.
Directed by: Louis Gasnier.
Starring: Carlos Gardel, Imperio Argentina, Vicente Padula
               and Jaime Devesa.

'CUESTA ABAJO'   1934

Produced by: Paramount.
Directed by: Louis Gasnier.
Starring: Carlos Gardel, Mona Maris, Vicente Padula, Anita
               del Campillo, Manuel Peluffo, Carlos Spaventa,
               Alfredo Le Pera and Jaime Devesa.

'EL TANGO EN BROADWAY'   1934

Produced by: Paramount.
Directed by: Louis Gasnier.
Starring: Carlos Gardel, Trini Ramos, Blanca Vischer,
               Vicente Padula and Jaime Devesa.

'CAZADORES DE ESTRELLAS'   1935

Produced by: Paramount.
Directed by: Norman Taurog and Theodore Reed.
Starring: Carlos Gardel, Jack Oakie, Ray Noble, the Vienna
               Boys' Choir, George Burns, Ethel Merman...

'EL DÍA QUE ME QUIERAS'   1935

Produced by: Paramount.
Directed by: John Reinhardt.
Starring: Carlos Gardel, Rosita Moreno, Tito Lusiardo,
               Manuel Peluffo...

'TANGO BAR'   1935

Produced by: Paramount.
Directed by: John Reinhardt.
Starring: Carlos Gardel, Rosita Moreno, Enrique de Rosas,
               Tito Lusiardo and José Luis Tortosa.

Mano a Mano sheet music. One of Gardel's greatest hits.

Gardel on the cover of two tango magazines
edited during his lifetime in Barcelona, Spain.

1928: Gardel poster by Paul Colin. This poster was used to promote Gardel's performances during his first Paris visit.

In 1931 Spanish movie magazine "Films Selectos"
offered its readers this Gardel poster.

Two posters used to promote Gardel's 1931 "Parade des Femmes" engagement at the Palace Theatre in Paris.

"Silencio" sheet music. Another great hit for Gardel.
Courtesy Saide Abdala Collection.

Promotional material for "Espérame" and "Melodía de Arrabal",
two films made in France.

In 1935, the film "Así cantaba Carlos Gardel"
was presented in Argentina.
It consisted of the songs Gardel was filmed singing in 1930.

Posters for
"El Dia que me Quieras"
and
"El Tango en Broadway",
two Gardel films
made in New York.

Gardel stamps from different countries.

DISCOGRAPHY

The charts below list Gardel's recordings in chronological order, according to the different systems (acoustic or electrical), record label, city and year. Each chart contains the master number, song title, musical genre, instrumental and vocal accompaniment (the latter when applicable), and the recording date.

Acoustic recordings for Columbia recorded by Gardel in Buenos Aires (1913)

Master	Title	Genre	Accompaniment	Date
56748	Sos Mi Tirador Plateao	Estilo	Gardel himself with guitar	1913
56749	Yo Sé Hacer	Cifra	"	1913
56750	La Mañanita	Estilo	"	1913
56752	A Mi Madre (Pobre Madre)	Estilo	"	1913
56753	Me Dejaste	Estilo	"	1913
56754	Mi China Cabrera (Palanganeando)	Estilo	"	1913
56755	El Sueño	Estilo	"	1913
56756	Pobre Flor	Estilo	"	1913
56757	La Mariposa	Estilo	"	1913
56758	Es en Vano	Canción	"	1913
56759	Brisas de la Tarde	Canción	"	1913
56760	El Almohadón	Vals	"	1913
56761	A Mitre	Vals	"	1913
56762	Pobre Mi Madre Querida	Canción	"	1913

Acoustic recordings for Odeón recorded, solo or duets with Razzano, in Buenos Aires (1917-1925)

Master	Title	Genre	Voices	Accompaniment	Date
28	Cantar Eterno	Canción	Gardel + Razzano	Guitar by Ricardo	1917
29	El Sol del 25	Gato	"	"	1917
30	Brisas	Canción	"	"	1917
31	La Huella	Canción	"	"	1917
32	La Criolla	Canción	"	"	1917
35	El Tirador Plateao	Estilo	Gardel	"	1917
36	El Moro	Canción	"	"	1917
37	La Mariposa	Estilo	"	"	1917
39	El Pangaré	Canción	"	"	1917
40	La China Fiera	Canción	Gardel + Razzano	"	1917
52	El Señuelo	Estilo	Gardel	"	1917
81	Una Rosa Para Mi Rosa	Canción	Gardel + Razzano	"	1917
82	Ya Canta el Gallo	Zamba	"	"	1917
86	Adiós Que Me Voy Llorando	Canción	"	"	1917
87	Puntana	Zamba	"	"	1917
88	Amargura	Estilo	Gardel	"	1917
89	Mi Noche Triste	Tango	"	"	1917
137	El Moro	Canción	Gardel + Razzano	Roberto Firpo Orchestra	1917
138	La Madrugada	Canción	"	Guitar by Ricardo	1917
139	Te Acordás	Zamba	"	"	1917
141	Lo que Fui	Estilo	Gardel	"	1917
29	Mis Perros	Bambuco	Gardel + Razzano	"	1919
30	Ay, Ay, Ay	Canción	"	"	1919
31	La Pastora	Canción	"	"	1919
32	A Mí Madre (Con los Amigos)	Canción	Gardel	"	1919
33	Flor de Fango	Tango	"	"	1919
55	Aurora	Vals	Gardel + Razzano	"	1919
56	Ay, Elena	Vals	"	"	1919
57	Sanjuanina de Mi Amor	Tonada	"	"	1919
58	La Yegüecita	Cueca	"	"	1919
59	Como Quiere la Madre a sus Hijos	Vals	Gardel	"	1919
60	Suena Guitarra Querida	Estilo	"	"	1919
66	El Cardo Azul	Estilo	"	"	1919
67	Qué Suerte la del Inglés	Estilo	"	"	1919
165	La Cordobesa	Zamba	Gardel + Razzano	"	1919

Master	Title	Genre	Voices	Accompaniment	Date
166	El Vagabundo	Bambuco	Gardel	Guitar by Ricardo + Razzano	1919
170	De Vuelta al Bulín	Tango	Gardel	"	1919
221	En Vano, En Vano	Vals	Gardel + Razzano	"	1920
222	Mi China	Fado	"	"	1920
223	Rumores	Bambuco	"	"	1920
224	Milongón	Milonga	"	"	1920
225	Mi Tierra	Zamba	"	"	1920
226	Ivette	Tango	Gardel	"	1920
227	Hay Una Virgen	Canción	"	"	1920
251	Pobre Madre	Estilo	"	"	1920
252	Amanecer	Cifra	"	"	1920
261	Linda Provincianita	Zamba	Gardel + Razzano	"	1920
262	Muñequita	Tango	Gardel	"	1920
326	Milonguita	Tango	"	"	1920
327	Mi Palomita	Tonada	Gardel + Razzano	"	1920
331	Por Que Te Quiero	Tonada	"	"	1920
332	Asómate a la Ventana	Serenata	Gardel	"	1920
339	Canto a la Selva	Canción	Gardel + Razzano	"	1920
340	Mi Caballo y Mi Mujer	Cueca	"	"	1920
341	Qué Querés con esa Cara	Tango	Gardel	"	1920
344	La Catedrática	Milonga	"	"	1920
353	Carne de Cabaret	Tango	"	"	1920
354	Pobre Paica	Tango	"	"	1920
375	Ausencia	Vals	Gardel + Razzano	"	1920
376	Pobre Gallo Bataraz	Estilo	Gardel	"	1920
442	Maragata	Tonada	"	"	1921
443	Margot	Tango	"	"	1921
444	Jujeña	Tonada	"	"	1921
448	Esas no Volverán	Canción	"	"	1921
449	Cielito Mío	Tango	"	"	1921
450	De Mi Tierra	Fado	"	"	1921
453	Zorro Gris	Tango	"	Guitars by Ricardo + Barbieri	1921
507	Campanita	Canción	Gardel + Razzano	"	1921
517	Pobre Mi Negra	Zamba	"	"	1921
556	La Tupungatina	Zamba	"	"	1921
557	Si Me Tendrá en su Memoria	Canción	"	"	1921
558	Eres Cruel	Estilo	Gardel	"	1921
559	Atardecer	Estilo	"	"	1921

Master	Title	Genre	Voices	Accompaniment	Date
560	El Pañuelito	Tango	Gardel	Guitars by Ricardo + Barbieri	1921
569	Rosarito la Serrana	Zamba	Gardel + Razzano	"	1921
570	Mirala Como Se Va	Tonada	"	"	1921
571	La Percanta está Triste	Tango	Gardel	"	1921
680	Chacarerita	Chacarera	Gardel + Razzano	"	1921
681	Con los Ojos del Alma	Gato	"	"	1921
682	Muñequita de Lujo	Tango	Gardel	"	1921
683	Qué has Hecho de Mi Cariño	Tango	"	"	1921
691	La Copa del Olvido	Tango	"	"	1921
722	Chinita Linda	Tonada	Gardel + Razzano	"	1921
746	El Sapo y la Comadreja	Tonada	"	"	1922
747	Contrastes	Vals	"	"	1922
748	Un Bailongo	Milonga	Gardel	"	1922
749	El Taita del Arrabal	Tango	"	"	1922
750	Los Indios	Tango	"	"	1922
751	Tu Diagnóstico	Vals	"	"	1922
755	Dos Cosas Te Pido	Tonada	Gardel + Razzano	"	1922
756	El Triunfo	Canción	"	"	1922
757	El Carretero	Canción	"	"	1922
758	Las Campanas	Vals	Gardel	"	1922
759	Qué Lindo Tiempo Aquel	Estilo	"	"	1922
760	Mi Ranchito	Canción	"	"	1922
784	Mi Estrella	Vals	Gardel + Razzano	"	1922
785	Donde Estará	Tonada	"	"	1922
786	Mi Pañuelo Bordao	Tonada	"	"	1922
787	La Cartita	Tango	Gardel	"	1922
788	Pobre Corazoncito	Tango	"	"	1922
789	La Cautiva	Tango	"	"	1922
790	Mi Bien Querido	Fado	"	"	1922
812	La Mascotita	Tango	"	"	1922
853	La Pueblerita	Zamba	Gardel + Razzano	"	1922
854	Pobre Vieja	Tango	Gardel	"	1922
871	Heroico Pays+ú	Canción	Gardel + Razzano	"	1922
872	Los Rosales se han Secao	Zamba	"	"	1922
873	Sufra	Tango	Gardel	"	1922
913	La Brisa	Tango	"	"	1922
914	Madre...!	Tango	"	"	1922
934	Hasta Besarla Llegué	Estilo	Gardel + Razzano	"	1922
935	Ámame Mucho	Tonada	"	"	1922
954	El Patotero Sentimental	Tango	Gardel	Guitars by Ricardo + Barbieri	1922

Master	Title	Genre	Voices Accompaniment	Date
977	Polvorín	Tango	" "	1922
978	La Provinciana	Tango	" "	1922
990	Co..co..ro..co	Zamba	" "	1922
991	El Tango de la Muerte	Tango	" "	1922
1027	El Corazón Me Robaste	Zamba	Gardel + Razzano "	1922
1028	Loca	Tango	Gardel "	1922
1029	Porotita	Tango	" "	1922
1069	Yo No Puedo Vivir Sin Amor	Shimmy	" "	1922
1070	Camarada	Tango	" "	1922
1080	La Maleva	Tango	" "	1922
1103	La Salteñita	Zamba	Gardel + Razzano "	1922
1104	Córdoba	Tango	Gardel "	1922
1105	Mis Flores Negras	Pasillo	" "	1922
1112	Nido de Amor	Tango	" "	1922
1129	El Pinche	Tango	" "	1923
1130	Como los Nardos en Flor	Tango	" "	1923
1131	Mi Manta Pampa	Zamba	" "	1923
1153	Mano a Mano	Tango	" "	1923
1154	Rosas de Otoño	Vals	" "	1923
1155	Mariposa	Tango	" "	1923
1156	Hacete Tonadillera	Tango	" "	1923
1175	El Paisano Contreras	Estilo	" "	1923
1176	Esas no Volverán	Canción	" "	1923
1207	Co..co..ro..co	Zamba	" "	1923
1222	La Chacarera	Tango	" "	1923
1223	Mi Refugio	Tango	" "	1923
1233	El Huérfano	Tango	" "	1923
1234	Buenos Aires	Tango	" "	1923
1264	La Muchacha	Tango	" "	1923
1308	La Cuyanita	Zamba	Gardel + Razzano "	1923
1309	Tendrás que Llorar	Vals	" "	1923
1310	Pobre Flores	Tango	Gardel "	1923
1311	Una Pena	Tango	" "	1923
1312	El Rey del Cabaret	Tango	" "	1923
1353	La Danza de las Libélulas	Canción	" "	1923
1354	Alma Porteña	Tango	" "	1923
1355	Viejecita Mía	Tango	" "	1923
1391	El Ramito	Tango	" "	1923
1396	Midinette Porteña	Tango	" "	1923
1397	Clarita	Tango	" "	1923
1398	Nubes de Humo	Tango	" "	1923
1438	Se Va... y Se Va	Tonada	Gardel + Razzano "	1923

Master	Title	Genre	Voices	Accompaniment	Date
1484	Celeste y Blanco	Tango	Gardel	Guitars by Ricardo + Barbieri	1923
1485	Padre Nuestro	Tango	"	"	1923
1486	Eche Otra Caña, Pulpero	Estilo	"	"	1923
1487	Pobre Milonga	Tango	"	"	1923
1567	Preciosa Mía	Tonada	Gardel + Razzano	"	1923
1568	Amor Perdido	Tango	Gardel	"	1923
1569	Tierrita	Tango	"	"	1923
1570	El Curdela	Tango	"	"	1923
1571	El Arroyito	Tango	"	"	1923
1572	Nerón	Shimmy	"	"	1923
1580	Rosal Viejo	Canción	Gardel + Razzano	"	1923
1581	Lo que Fuiste	Tango	Gardel	"	1923
1582	Mentías	Tango	"	"	1923
1588	Los Ojazos de Mi Negra	Zamba	Gardel + Razzano	"	1923
1589	La Tacuarita	Zamba	"	"	1923
1590	Tierra del Fuego	Tango	Gardel	"	1923
1591	Cartitas Perfumadas	Tango	"	"	1923
1592	Desengaño	Tango	"	"	1923
1597	Como Agoniza la Flor	Canción	Gardel + Razzano	"	1923
1598	Tu Vieja Ventana	Vals	"	"	1923
1599	Desdichas	Tango	Gardel	"	1923
1600	Sobre el Pucho	Tango	"	"	1923
1601	Triste Entrerriano	Triste	"	"	1923
1602	China Hereje	Estilo	"	"	1923
1764	Sacate la Caretita	Tango	"	"	1924
1765	El Consentido	Tango	"	"	1924
1769	Príncipe	Tango	"	"	1924
1770	Sombras	Tango	"	"	1924
1771	Francesita	Tango	"	"	1924
1777	Congojas	Tango	"	"	1924
1778	Desolación	Tango	"	"	1924
1779	Se Acuerdan, Muchachos	Tango	"	"	1924
1780	Perdóname, Señor	Tango	"	"	1924
1781	Nunca Más	Tango	"	"	1924
1794	Pobre Amigo	Tango	"	"	1924
1795	Tranco a Tranco	Tango	"	"	1924
1809	Primavera de colores	Estilo	"	"	1924
1810	Tut-ankh-amon	Camel-trot	"	"	1924
1811	Cascabelito	Tango	"	"	1924
1812	De Flor en Flor	Tango	"	"	1924
1813	Sueño Marchito	Tango	"	"	1924
1849	Milonga Fina	Tango	"	"	1924

Master	Title	Genre	Voices	Accompaniment	Date
1850	La Enmascarada	Tango	Gardel	Guitars by Ricardo + Barbieri	1924
1851	Talán, Talán	Tango	"	"	1924
1852	El Templo de Venus	Shimmy	"	"	1924
1853	El Alma que Siente	Tango	"	"	1924
1854	Il Píccolo Navío	Tango	"	"	1924
1861	Yo Tuyo Soy, Tuyo Es Mi Amor	Vidalita	"	"	1924
1862	Adiós, Que Te Vaya Bien	Zamba	"	"	1924
2044	El Besito	Tango	"	"	1924
2045	La Vuelta de Rocha	Tango	"	"	1924
2126	Aunque Me Cuesta La Vida	Zamba	"	"	1924
2127	Poupeè de Estambul	Shimmy	"	"	1924
2128	Macachín Flor de los Llanos	Tango	"	"	1924
2129	La Cabeza del Italiano	Tango	"	"	1924
2137	Pobre Madrecita	Tango	"	"	1924
2190	Argentina	Tango	"	"	1924
2191	Misterio	Tango	"	"	1924
2192	Mía	Tango	"	"	1924
2197	La Garçonniere	Tango	"	Francisco Canaro Orch	1924
2198	Como Agoniza la Flor	Canción	"	"	1924
2260	Claveles Mendocinos	Zamba	Gardel + Razzano	Guitars by Ricardo +Barbieri	1924
2261	Tucumana	Zamba	Gardel	"	1924
2262	No le Digas que la Quiero	Tango	"	"	1924
2275	Hollín	Tango	"	"	1924
2276	La Mentirosa	Tango	"	"	1924
2277	Por un Tango	Tango	"	"	1924
2278	Destino	Tango	"	"	1924
2279	Todo Corazón	Tango	"	"	1924
2289	Oh! Paris	Tango	"	Francisco Canaro Orch	1924
2289	Oh! Paris	Foxtrot	"	Guitars by Ricardo + Barbieri	1924
2290	Beso Ingrato	Tango	"	"	1924
2290	Beso Ingrato	Tango	"	Francisco Canaro Orch	1924
2291	La Sulamita	Shimmy	"	Guitars by Ricardo + Barbieri	1924
2292	Si Supieras (La Cumparsita)	Tango	"	"	1924
2388	Aquella palomita	Canción	Gardel + Razzano	"	1924
2389	Aromas	Tango	Gardel	"	1924
2390	Tesorito	Tango	"	"	1924
2391	El Olivo	Tango	"	"	1924
2434	Sin Madre	Tango	"	"	1924
2435	La Mina del Ford	Tango	"	"	1924

Master	Title	Genre	Voices	Accompaniment	Date
2436	Pero hay una Melena	Foxtrot	Gardel	Guitars by Ricardo + Barbieri	1924
2491	Griseta	Tango	"	"	1924
2530	Machaza Mi Suerte	Zamba	Gardel + Razzano	"	1925
2531	Por el Camino	Tango	Gardel	"	1925
2532	Galleguita	Tango	"	"	1925
2537	El Once	Tango	"	"	1925
2538	Sentimiento Gaucho	Tango	"	"	1925
2551	Amigazo	Tango	"	"	1925
2552	Añorando	Tango	"	"	1925
2553	Por Ultima Vez	Tango	"	"	1925
2567	Pa´ que Te Acordés	Tango	"	"	1925
2568	Caminito del Taller	Tango	"	"	1925
2586	Para Quererte Nací	Cifra	"	"	1925
2587	Mala	Tango	"	"	1925
2594	Tuyo	Tango	"	"	1925
2595	Mis Espuelas	Estilo	"	"	1925
2640	Circe	Shimmy	"	"	1925
2623	La Cuyanita	Tango	"	"	1925
2708	La Choyana	Chacarera	Gardel + Razzano	"	1925
2709	Del Infierno Adelante	Gato	"	"	1925
2710	Reyes del Aire	Shimmy	Gardel	"	1925
2728	Caricias	Tango	"	"	1925
2729	Organito de la Tarde	Tango	"	"	1925
2730	Oro y Seda	Tango	"	"	1925
2770	Mano Mora	Tango	"	"	1925
2771	Honolulu	Shimmy	"	"	1925
2786	Aquella Noche	Tango	"	"	1925
2787	Sonia	Balada	"	"	1925
2811	Adelante	Marcha	"	"	1925
2823	Puentecito	Tango	"	"	1925
2824	Mi Guitarra	Tango	"	"	1925
2854	Guaminí	Tango	"	"	1925
2855	Salve, Patria	Estilo	"	"	1925
2856	Pasan las Horas	Vals	"	"	1925
2901	El Zaino Colorado	Estilo	"	"	1925
2902	La Canción del Ukelele	Foxtrot	"	"	1925
2903	Flor de Cardo	Tango	"	"	1925
2962	El Picaflor	Tonada	Gardel + Razzano	"	1925
2963	Maniquí	Tango	Gardel	"	1925
2964	Trapito	Tango	"	"	1925
2965	Hola... Señorita	Shimmy	"	"	1925
3000	Llora Corazón (Angustia)	Vals	Gardel + Razzano	"	1925

Master	Title	Genre	Voices	Accompaniment	Date
3009	Volveme el Cariñito	Zamba	Gardel	Guitars by Ricardo + Barbieri	1925
3010	Acuarelita de Arrabal	Tango	"	"	1925
3011	Silbando	Tango	"	"	1925
3012	Por el Llano	Tango	"	"	1925
3033	Cañaveral	Zamba	Gardel + Razzano	"	1925
3034	Mentiras	Tango	Gardel	"	1925
3035	Pobre Muñequita	Tango	"	"	1925
3049	Oh! Penas Mías	Tango	"	"	1925
3050	Cicatrices	Tango	"	"	1925
3072	Langosta	Tango	"	"	1925
3073	Soñando	Tango	"	"	1925
3074	Tus Violetas	Tango	"	"	1925
3151	Tango Porteño	Tango	"	"	1925
3152	Por Ella	Tango	"	"	1925
3153	Callecita de Mi Barrio	Tango	"	"	1925
3169	Mi Ambición	Vals	Gardel + Razzano	"	1925
3170	Entrá Nomás	Tango	Gardel	"	1925
3171	Sonsa	Tango	"	"	1925
3217	Milonguera	Tango	"	"	1925
3218	Muchachita de Montmartre	Tango	"	"	1925
3219	Una Noche en "El Garrón"	Tango	"	"	1925
3237	Porteña del Rosedal	Zamba	Gardel + Razzano	"	1925
3238	El Anillo	Zamba	Gardel	"	1925
3275	Ave Cantora	Tango	"	"	1925
3276	Fea	Tango	"	"	1925
3277	Idilio Campero	Tango	"	"	1925
3278	Adiós Para Siempre	Tango	"	"	1925
3285	Viejo Rincón	Tango	"	"	1925
3286	Corto de Genio	Tango	"	"	1925
3287	Jirón de Pampa	Tango	"	"	1925
3288	Fea	Tango	"	Osvaldo Fresedo Orchestra	1925
3289	Perdón Viejita	Tango	"	"	1925
3290	El Triunfo	Danza	Gardel + Razzano	Guitars by Ricardo + Barbieri	1925
3291	Dejá el Conventillo	Tango	Gardel	"	1925
3292	Quejas del Alma	Tango	"	"	1925
3293	Cordobesita	Zamba	"	"	1925
3294	Es Tanto lo que Te Quiero	Tonada	"	"	1925

Electrical Recordings for Odeón recorded by Gardel in Barcelona (1925-1926)

Master	Title	Genre	Accompaniment	Date
So 3815	Echaste Buena	Tango	Guitar by Ricardo	12/26/1925
So 3816	Mi Querer	Tango	"	12/26/1925
So 3817	Sueños	Tango	"	12/26/1925
So 3818	Amor Gran Buda	Shimmy	"	12/26/1925
So 3819	Pompas	Tango	"	12/27/1925
So 3820	Raza Noble	Tango	"	12/27/1925
So 3822	Pedime lo que Querés	Tango	"	12/27/1925
So 3823	Yo Te Bendigo	Tango	"	12/27/1925
So 3824	Pobre Chica	Tango	"	12/27/1925
So 3825	El Bulín de la Calle Ayacucho	Tango	"	12/27/1925
So 3826	Maldita Visión	Tango	"	12/27/1925
So 3827	Leguisamo Sólo!	Tango	"	12/27/1925
So 3828	Oiga Amigo	Tango	"	12/27/1925
So 3839	El Alma de la Calle	Tango	"	01/08/1926
So 3840	Desilusión	Tango	"	01/08/1926
So 3841	Chola	Tango	"	01/08/1926
So 3842	Corazón de Arrabal	Tango	"	01/08/1926
So 3850	El Tatuaje	Tango	"	01/09/1926
So 3851	Malevito	Tango	"	01/09/1926
So 3855	Dolor	Tango	"	01/09/1926
So 3856	Trago Amargo	Tango	"	01/09/1926

Acoustic recordings for Odeón recorded by Gardel in Buenos Aires (1926)

Master	Title	Genre	Accompaniment	Date
3808	Mi Querer	Tango	Guitars by Ricardo + Barbieri	1926
3809	Trago Amargo	Tango	"	1926
3810	Oiga Amigo	Tango	"	1926
3811	El Alma de la Calle	Tango	"	1926
3812	Maldita Visión	Tango	"	1926
3813	El Bulín de la Calle Ayacucho	Tango	"	1926
3884	El Brujo	Tango	"	1926
3885	Tiempos Viejos	Tango	"	1926
3886	El Tatuaje	Tango	"	1926
3887	La Cieguita	Tango	"	1926
3888	Caferata	Tango	"	1926
3925	La He Visto Con Otro	Tango	"	1926
3926	La Tristeza del Bulín	Tango	"	1926
3927	Valencia	Pasodoble	"	1926
3928	Desilusión	Tango	"	1926

Master	Title	Genre	Accompaniment	Date
3929	No Te Quiero Más	Tango	Guitars by Ricardo + Barbieri	1926
3930	Copen la Banca	Tango	"	1926
3963	Chola	Tango	"	1926
3964	Tus Besos Fueron Míos	Tango	"	1926
3965	Siga el Corso	Tango	"	1926
3966	El Lazo	Estilo	"	1926
4009	Se fue Mateo	Tango	"	1926
4010	Bésame en la Boca	Tango	"	1926
4011	Tu Mirada	Tango	"	1926
4012	Que Lindo es el Shimmy	Shimmy	"	1926
4013	La Milonga	Tango	"	1926
4075	Por Qué No Has Venido	Tango	"	1926
4076	Caminito	Tango	"	1926
4077	Yo Te Bendigo	Tango	"	1926
4078	Pobre Chica	Tango	"	1926
4099	Calandria	Tango	"	1926
4100	Juguete de Placer	Tango	"	1926
4127	Nena	Tango	"	1926
4128	Ave Sin Rumbo	Tango	"	1926
4129	Aquel Cuartito de la Pensión	Tango	"	1926
4130	Noches de Colón	Tango	"	1926
4131	Mi Mocosita	Tango	"	1926
4253	A Media Noche	Tango	"	1926
4254	Una Lágrima	Tango	"	1926
4286	Intimas	Tango	"	1926
4287	Oro Muerto (Jirón Porteño)	Tango	"	1926
4336	Chacarerita del Norte	Chacarera	"	1926
4337	Mi Suegra No Me Quiere	Gato	"	1926
4338	A Media Luz	Tango	"	1926
4352	Pa Qué Más	Tango	"	1926
4353	Rosas Rojas	Tango	"	1926
4354	Qué Linda es la Vida	Waltz	"	1926
4355	Coquetita	Tango	"	1926
4493	Muñeca	Tango	"	1926
4494	Francia	Tango	"	1926
4495	Pobre Corazón Mío	Tango	"	1926
4496	Calavera Viejo	Tango	"	1926
4550	Señor	Tango	"	1926
4551	Cariñito Mío	Tango	"	1926
4552	Como las Margaritas	Estilo	"	1926
4585	El Ciruja	Tango	"	1926
4588	Puñadito de Sal	Pasodoble	"	1926

Electrical Recordings for Odeón recorded by Gardel
in Buenos Aires (1926)

Master	Title	Genre	Accompaniment	Date
1	Puñadito de Sal	Pasodoble	Guitars by Ricardo + Barbieri	11/08/1926
2	Mi Diosa	Tango	"	11/08/1926
3	Del Barrio de las Latas	Tango	"	11/08/1926
9	Calavera Viejo	Tango	"	11/10/1926
26	No Me Tires con la Tapa de la Olla	Tango	"	11/15/1926

Acoustic recordings for Odeón recorded by Gardel
in Buenos Aires (1926)

Master	Title	Genre	Accompaniment	Date
4589	Puñadito de Sal	Pasodoble	Guitars by Ricardo + Barbieri	11/26/1926
4590	Calavera Viejo	Tango	"	11/26/1926
4591	Mi Diosa	Tango	"	11/26/1926
4592	Del Barrio de las Latas	Tango	"	11/26/1926
4593	No Me Tires con la Tapa de la Olla	Tango	"	11/26/1926
4594	Dicha Pasada	Tango	"	11/26/1926

Electrical Recordings for Odeón recorded by Gardel
in Buenos Aires (1926-1927)

Master	Title	Genre	Accompaniment	Date
88	Ya Pa´ Qué	Tango	Guitars by Ricardo + Barbieri	11/30/1926
89	Puñadito de Sal	Pasodoble	"	11/30/1926
90	Del Barrio de las Latas	Tango	"	11/30/1926
91	Aquella Cantina de la Ribera	Tango	"	11/30/1926
92	Del Barrio de las Latas	Tango	"	12/01/1926
93	Dicha Pasada	Tango	"	12/01/1926
94	Mi Diosa	Tango	"	12/01/1926
118	Corrientes	Tango	"	12/04/1926
119	Noche Fría	Tango	"	12/04/1926
120	El Pibe	Tango	"	12/04/1926
121	La Violetera	Tango	"	12/04/1926
137	Viejo Amor	Tango	"	12/09/1926
173	Soy una Fiera	Milonga	"	12/16/1926
192	Páginas de Amor	Tango	"	12/17/1926
193	Bajo Belgrano	Tango	"	12/17/1926
194	Llegué a Ladrón por Amarte	Tango	"	12/17/1926
195	Rumores	Tango	"	12/17/1926
224	Ansias de Amor	Tango	"	12/24/1926
225	Normiña	Tango	"	12/24/1926
226	Llora Hermano	Tango	"	12/24/1926

Master	Title	Genre	Accompaniment	Date
275	Abuelito	Tango	Guitars by Ricardo + Barbieri	12/31/1926
276	Gorriones	Tango	"	12/31/1926
277	Perdonada	Tango	"	12/31/1926
363	Compañero	Tango	"	02/06/1927
383	Perdonada	Tango	"	02/17/1927
384	Páginas de Amor	Tango	"	02/17/1927
385	Pan Comido	Tango	"	02/18/1927
386	Barrio Reo	Tango	"	02/18/1927
387	¿Por Dónde Andará?	Tango	"	02/18/1927
388	Y Era Buena	Tango	"	02/18/1927
471	Hopa, Hopa, Hopa	Canción	"	03/12/1927
472	Sos de Chiclana	Tango	"	03/12/1927
473	La Violetera	Tango	"	03/12/1927
541	Gajito de Cedrón	Chacarera	"	03/30/1927
542	El Sueño	Estilo	"	03/30/1927
543	Bulincito de Mi Vida	Tango	"	03/30/1927
544	Carnaval	Tango	"	03/30/1927
545	Se Acabaron los Otarios	Tango	"	03/30/1927
546	Che, Mariano	Tango	"	03/30/1927
719	Federación	Tango	"	05/05/1927
720	Besos que Matan	Tango	"	05/05/1927
721	Insomnio	Canción	"	05/05/1927
722	Arrabalero	Tango	"	05/05/1927
788	Muñeca de Carne	Tango	"	05/27/1927
789	Araca Corazón	Tango	"	05/27/1927
919	La Ultima Copa	Tango	"	06/14/1927
953	La Entrerriana	Vals	"	06/21/1927
954	Mala Entraña	Tango	"	06/21/1927
955	Muchachos, Me Caso	Tango	"	06/21/1927
1001	El Poncho del Amor	Tango	"	07/08/1927
1002	Ventanita de Arrabal	Tango	"	07/08/1927
1003	Un Tropezón	Tango	"	07/22/1927
1004	Gimiendo	Tango	"	07/08/1927
1041	A la Luz del Candil	Tango	"	07/20/1927
1042	Micifuz	Tango	"	07/20/1927
1043	Rosas de Abril	Vals	"	07/20/1927
1060	Amurado	Tango	"	07/22/1927
1061	Isla de Flores	Tango	"	07/22/1927
1062	Yo Te Imploro (El Trovero)	Vals	"	07/22/1927
1109	Caminito	Tango	"	07/29/1927
1110	Una Tarde	Tango	"	07/29/1927
1111	Sonrisas	Shimmy	"	07/30/1927
1112	Salto Mortal	Tango	"	07/30/1927

Master	Title	Genre	Accompaniment	Date
1214	Farolito Viejo	Tango	Guitars by Ricardo + Barbieri	08/20/1927
1215	La Gayola	Tango	"	08/20/1927
1216	Glorias	Tango	"	08/20/1927
1370	Alma de Loca	Tango	"	09/23/1927
1371	Vida Amarga	Tango	"	09/23/1927
1372	Pobre Colombina	Tango	"	09/23/1927
1373	Te Fuiste, Hermano!	Tango	"	09/23/1927
1374	Pompas	Tango	"	09/23/1927
1375	Leguisamo, Sólo!	Tango	"	09/23/1927
1455	Yo Te Perdono	Tango	"	10/06/1927
1456	Viejo Curda	Tango	"	10/06/1927
1457	Ebrio	Tango	"	10/06/1927
1458	Compadrón	Tango	"	10/06/1927
1459	No Llores Más	Tango	"	10/06/1927
1460	Sonia	Balada Rusa	"	10/06/1927
1497	Perfume de Mujer	Tango	"	10/22/1927
1604	Copetín, Vos Sos Mi Hermano	Tango	"	10/22/1927
1605	Noche de Reyes	Tango	"	10/22/1927
1606	Queja Indiana	Tango	"	10/22/1927
1607	Fiesta Criolla	Tango	"	10/22/1927
1608	El Mal Que Me Hiciste	Tango	"	10/22/1927
1609	Tierra Hermana	Tango	"	10/22/1927

Electrical Recordings for Odeón recorded by Gardel in Barcelona (1928)

Master	Title	Genre	Accompaniment	Date
So 4550	¿Cuando Volverás?	Tango	Guitars by Ricardo + Barbieri	01/09/1928
So 4551	Cotorrita de la Suerte	Tango	"	01/09/1928
So 4552	Volvé Mi Negra	Tango	"	01/09/1928
So 4553	Qué Vachaché	Tango	"	01/09/1928
So 4554	Así Canto Yo	Tango	"	01/09/1928
So 4555	Puentecito de Plata	Tango	"	01/09/1928
So 4556	Meditando	Tango	"	01/09/1928
So 4557	El Tabernero	Tango	"	01/09/1928
So 4558	Y Reías Como Loca	Tango	"	01/09/1928
So 4559	De Tardecita	Tango	"	01/09/1928
So 4560	Y si la Ves Dale un Beso	Tango	"	01/10/1928
So 4561	Lobo de Mar (Mar Bravío)	Tango	"	01/10/1928
So 4562	La Cieguita	Tango	"	01/10/1928
So 4563	Siga el Corso	Tango	"	01/10/1928
So 4564	Si Supieras (La Cumparsita)	Tango	"	01/10/1928
So 4565	Tu Vieja Ventana	Vals	"	01/10/1928

Master	Title	Genre	Accompaniment	Date
So 4566	Mano a Mano	Tango	Guitars by Ricardo + Barbieri	01/10/1928
So 4567	No Llores Más	Tango	"	01/10/1928
So 4568	Por un Cariño	Tango	"	01/10/1928
So 4569	Tristeza Gaucha	Estilo	"	01/10/1928
So 4626	La Borrachera del Tango	Tango	"	01/14/1928
So 4627	La Reja	Tango	"	01/14/1928
So 4628	La Gloria del Aguila	Tango	"	01/14/1928
So 4629	Resignate, Hermano	Tango	"	01/14/1928
So 4630	Dandy	Tango	"	01/14/1928
So 4631	Traicionera	Tango	"	01/14/1928
So 4632	Reproches	Tango	"	01/14/1928
So 4633	De Puro Guapo	Tango	"	01/14/1928
So 4635	La Sulamita	Shimmy	"	01/14/1928
So 4636	Pato	Tango	"	01/14/1928

Electrical Recordings for Odeón recorded by Gardel in Buenos Aires (1928)

Master	Title	Genre	Accompaniment	Date
2789	Resignate, Hermano	Tango	Guitars by Ricardo + Barbieri	06/20/1928
2790	Mar Bravío (Lobo de Mar)	Tango	"	06/20/1928
2791	La Borrachera del Tango	Tango	"	06/20/1928
2792	La Reja	Tango	"	06/20/1928
2793	Dandy	Tango	"	06/20/1928
2794	Reproche	Tango	"	06/20/1928
2795	De Puro Guapo	Tango	"	06/20/1928
2796	Qué Vachaché	Tango	"	06/20/1928
2829	Esta Noche Me Emborracho	Tango	"	06/26/1928
2830	Che Papusa, Oí	Tango	"	06/26/1928
2831	Adiós Muchachos	Tango	"	06/26/1928
2832	No Te Engañes Corazón	Tango	"	06/26/1928
2833	Siga el Corso	Tango	"	06/26/1928
2834	La Sulamita	Shimmy	"	06/26/1928
2862	El Carrerito	Tango	"	07/06/1928
2863	Lechuza	Tango	"	07/06/1928
2864	Chorra	Tango	"	07/06/1928
2865	La Hija de Japonesita	Foxtrot	"	07/06/1928
2922	Chorra	Tango	"	07/23/1928
2923	Manos Brujas	Foxtrot	"	07/23/1928
2965	Canción de Cuna	Tango	"	08/02/1928
2966	Las Madreselvas	Zamba	"	08/02/1928
2967	Por el Camino	Zamba	"	08/02/1928
2968	Corazoncito	Tango	"	08/02/1928
3039	En un Pueblito de España	Vals	"	08/16/1928

Master	Title	Genre	Accompaniment	Date
3040	Cuando Llora La Milonga	Tango	Guitars by Ricardo + Barbieri	08/17/1928
3120	En un Pueblito de España	Vals	"	09/06/1928
3121	Mano Cruel	Tango	"	09/06/1928
3122	Che, Bartolo	Tango	"	09/06/1928

Electrical Recordings for Odeón recorded by Gardel in Paris (1928-1929)

Master	Title	Genre	Accompaniment	Date
Ki 1849	Piedad	Tango	Guitars by Ricardo, Barbieri + Aguilar	10/11/1928
Ki 1850	Te Aconsejo Que Me Olvides	Tango	"	10/11/1928
Ki 1851	Alma en Pena	Tango	"	10/11/1928
Ki 1852	Duelo criollo	Tango	"	10/11/1928
Ki 1853	Noviecita Mía	Tango	"	10/11/1928
Ki 1854	Fierro Chifle	Tango	"	10/11/1928
Ki 1855	El Carretero	Canción	"	10/11/1928
Ki 1856	Ramona	Vals	"	10/11/1928
Ki 1880	Cuando Llora La Milonga	Tango	"	10/20/1928
Ki 1881	Traicionera	Tango	"	10/20/1928
Ki 1882	Bandoneón Arrabalero	Tango	"	10/20/1928
Ki 1884	Cualquier Cosa	Tango	"	10/20/1928
Ki 1885	Rosas de Otoño	Vals	"	10/20/1928
Ki 1926	Allá en la Ribera	Tango	"	10/27/1928
Ki 1927	Refucilos	Tango	"	10/27/1928
Ki 1928	Barra Querida	Tango	"	10/27/1928
Ki 1929	Mentirosa	Tango	"	10/27/1928
Ki 1974	La Reina del Tango	Tango	"	11/27/1928
Ki 1975	Lo han Visto con Otra	Tango	"	11/27/1928
Ki 1976	Pobre Pato	Tango	"	11/27/1928
Ki 2054	No Te Engañes, Corazón	Tango	"	12/15/1928
Ki 2055	Tengo Miedo	Tango	"	12/15/1928
Ki 2056	Patadura	Tango	"	12/15/1928
Ki 2057	Aquel Muchacho Triste	Tango	"	12/15/1928
Ki 2058	Medianoche	Tango	"	12/15/1928
Ki 2059	Todavía hay Otarios	Tango	"	12/15/1928
Ki 2060	Mano Cruel	Tango	"	12/15/1928
Ki 2073	Farabute	Tango	"	12/15/1928
Ki 2074	Barrio Viejo	Tango	"	12/22/1928
Ki 2075	La Muchacha del Circo	Tango	"	12/22/1928
Ki 2076	Senda Florida	Tango	"	12/22/1928
Ki 2077	Manos Brujas	Foxtrot	"	12/22/1928
Ki 2078	Añoranzas	Vals	"	12/22/1928
Ki 2079	Pobre Mi Gaucha	Cifra	"	12/22/1928

Master	Title	Genre	Accompaniment	Date
Ki 2080	Nelly	Vals	Guitars by Ricardo, Barbieri + Aguilar	12/22/1928
Ki 2081	Paseo de Julio	Tango	"	12/22/1928
Ki 2241	Se Llama Mujer	Tango	"	03/01/1929
Ki 2242	Malevaje	Tango	"	03/01/1929
Ki 2243	Aquel Tapado de Armiño	Tango	"	03/01/1929
Ki 2244	Cruz de Palo	Tango	"	03/01/1929
Ki 2245	Trenzas Negras	Tango	"	03/01/1929
Ki 2246	Como Todas	Vals	"	03/01/1929
Ki 2247	Haragán	Tango	"	03/01/1929
Ki 2248	A Contramano	Tango	"	03/01/1929
Ki 2249	Por Que Me Das Dique	Tango	"	03/01/1929
Ki 2250	Echando Mala	Tango	"	03/01/1929
Ki 2336	Estampilla	Tango	"	04/06/1929
Ki 2337	Cachadora	Tango	"	04/06/1929
Ki 2338	Seguí Mi Consejo	Tango	"	04/06/1929
Ki 2339	Primero Yo	Tango	"	04/06/1929

Electrical Recordings for Odeón recorded by Gardel in Buenos Aires (1929)

Master	Title	Genre	Accompaniment	Date
4260	Barrio Viejo	Tango	Guitars by Aguilar + Barbieri	06/20/1929
4261	Aquel Tapado de Armiño	Tango	"	06/20/1929
4262	Estampilla	Tango	"	06/20/1929
4263	Cachadora	Tango	"	06/20/1929
4264	Malevaje	Tango	"	06/20/1929
4265	Tango, Te Cambiaron la Pinta	Tango	"	06/20/1929
4266	Primero Yo	Tango	"	06/20/1929
4270	Cariñito	Tango	"	06/20/1929
4271	Haragán	Tango	"	06/21/1929
4272	Seguí Mi Consejo	Tango	"	06/21/1929
4273	Callejera	Tango	"	06/21/1929
4274	Sevilla	Pasodoble	"	06/21/1929
4275	Te Fuiste, Ja, Ja	Tango	"	06/21/1929
4276	Tan Grande y Tan Zonzo	Tango	"	06/21/1929
4290	Como Todas	Vals	"	06/28/1929
4291	Tengo Miedo	Tango	"	06/28/1929
4292	Aquel Muchacho Triste	Tango	"	06/28/1929
4293	Cabecita Negra	Tango	"	06/28/1929
4294	Ríe, Payaso	Tango	"	06/28/1929
4295	La Casita está Triste	Tango	"	06/28/1929
4296	Muñeca Brava	Tango	"	06/28/1929

Master	Title	Genre	Accompaniment	Date
4390	Milonguera	Tango	Guitars by Aguilar + Barbieri	07/22/1929
4391	Cruz de Palo	Tango	"	07/22/1929
4392	Echando Mala	Tango	"	07/22/1929
4393	Flor campera	Tango	"	07/22/1929
4449	Maryflor	Vals	"	08/08/1929
4450	Mascotita de Marfil	Vals	"	08/08/1929
4451	La Divina Dama	Vals	"	08/08/1929
4452	Uno y Uno	Tango	"	08/08/1929
4453	Paseo de Julio	Tango	"	08/08/1929
4454	Largue a esa Música	Tango	"	08/08/1929
4463	¡Qué Fenómeno!	Tango	"	08/12/1929
4464	Machete	Tango	"	08/12/1929
4465	Dos en Uno	Tango	"	08/12/1929
4513	La Divina Dama	Vals	"	08/25/1929
4514	Yo Beso Vuestra Mano, Señora	Canción	"	08/25/1929
4515	Culpas Ajenas	Tango	"	08/25/1929
4566	Margaritas	Tango	"	09/10/1929
4567	Yo También Como Tu	Tango	"	09/10/1929
4568	Manuelita	Vals	"	09/10/1929
4581	Lloró como una Mujer	Tango	"	09/12/1929
4582	El Barbijo	Tango	"	09/12/1929
4583	Prisionero	Tango	"	09/12/1929
4584	Victoria	Tango	"	09/12/1929
4594	Misa de Once	Tango	"	09/14/1929
4693	Esta Vida es Puro Grupo	Tango	"	10/11/1929
4694	Bailarín Compadrito	Tango	"	10/11/1929
4742	Alicia	Vals	"	10/23/1929
4743	La Virgen del Perdón	Vals	"	10/23/1929
4744	Virgencita de Pompeya	Tango	"	10/23/1929
4745	P´al cambalache	Tango	"	10/23/1929
4746	Palermo	Tango	"	10/23/1929
4747	Te Odio	Tango	"	10/23/1929
4748	Mentiras Criollas	Tango	"	10/23/1929
4859	De Todo Te Olvidas	Tango	"	11/12/1929
4860	Pensalo Bien	Tango	"	11/12/1929
4861	Alicia	Tango	"	11/12/1929
4867	¿Por Qué Soy Reo?	Tango	"	11/13/1929
4868	Mamita	Tango	"	11/13/1929
5031	Barajando	Tango	"	12/11/1929
5032	Calor de Hogar	Tango	"	12/11/1929
5033	Tango Argentino	Tango	"	12/11/1929
5034	Misterio	Canción	"	12/11/1929

Master	Title	Genre	Accompaniment	Date
5035	Que se Vayan	Tango	Guitars by Aguilar + Barbieri	12/11/1929
5036	Mamita	Tango	"	12/11/1929
5102	Trianera	Pasodoble	"	12/18/1929
5103	Ofrenda Gaucha	Estilo	"	12/18/1929
5104	Siéntese, Che Hermano	Tango	"	12/18/1929
5118	Recordándote	Tango	"	12/20/1929
5119	Tras Cartón	Tango	"	12/20/1929
5120	El Cimarrón del Estribo	Canción	"	12/20/1929
5121	La Mariposa	Estilo	"	12/20/1929
5151	Garabatos de Mujer	Tango	"	12/31/1929
5152	Amor Pagano	Vals	"	12/31/1929
5153	El Cardo Azul	Estilo	"	12/31/1929
5154	De Salto y Carta	Tango	"	12/31/1929

Electrical Recordings for Odeón recorded by the Gardel-Razzano duo in Buenos Aires (1929)

Master	Title	Genre	Voices	Accompaniment	Date
5155	Claveles Mendocinos	Zamba	Gardel + Razzano	Guitars by Aguilar + Barbieri	12/31/1929
5156	Serrana Impía	Zamba	"	"	12/31/1929

Electrical Recordings for Odeón recorded by Gardel in Buenos Aires (1930)

Master	Title	Genre	Accompaniment	Date
5196	Misterio	Canción	Guitars by Aguilar + Barbieri	03/10/1930
5197	Solo se Quiere una Vez	Tango	"	03/10/1930
5198	El Cardo Azul	Estilo	"	03/10/1930
5262	Juventud	Tango	Guitars by Barbieri, Aguilar + Riverol	03/20/1930
5263	Corazón de Papel	Tango	"	03/20/1930
5264	Palomita Blanca	Vals	"	03/20/1930
5265	Aromas del Cairo	Vals	"	03/20/1930
5266	Buenos Aires	Tango	"	03/20/1930
5266	Buenos Aires	Tango	Guitars, violin and piano	04/01/1930
5326	Yo Nací para Ti, Tu Serás para Mí	Foxtrot	"	04/01/1930
5326	"	Foxtrot	Guitars by Barbieri, Aguilar + Riverol	04/24/1930
5327	Aromas del Cairo	Vals	Guitars, double bass, and piano	04/01/1930
5328	Buenos Aires	Tango	"	04/01/1930
5329	Aquellas Farras	Tango	"	04/01/1930
5330	Viejo Smocking	Tango	"	04/01/1930

Master	Title	Genre	Accompaniment	Date
5330	Viejo Smocking	Tango	Guitars by Barbieri, Aguilar + Riverol	04/24/1930
5402	Lo han Visto con Otra	Tango	"	04/10/1930
5402	Lo han Visto con Otra	Tango	Guitars, violin and piano	04/15/1930
5428	Senda Florida	Tango	Guitars by Barbieri, Aguilar + Riverol	04/15/1930
5429	Cartas Viejas Tango	Tango	"	04/15/1930
5430	Viejo Jardín	Vals	"	04/15/1930
5449	Mi Noche Triste	Tango	"	04/24/1930
5450	Vieja Recoba	Tango	"	04/24/1930
5451	Pajarito	Tango	"	04/24/1930
5470	Primero Campaneala	Tango	"	04/29/1930
5471	La Mariposa	Estilo	"	04/29/1930
5472	Pobre Gallo Bataraz	Estilo	"	04/29/1930
5488	Almagro	Tango	"	05/01/1930
5489	Matala	Tango	"	05/01/1930
5490	Contramarca	Tango	"	05/01/1930
5600	Dicen que Dicen	Tango	"	05/20/1930
5601	Una Lagrima	Vals	"	05/20/1930
5602	Enfundá la Mandolina	Tango	"	05/20/1930
5603	Insomnio	Canción	"	05/20/1930
5604	Amigazo	Tango	"	05/20/1930
5615	A Mí Madre (Con los Amigos)	Canción	"	05/20/1930
5616	El Sol del 25	Gato	"	05/20/1930
5617	Rosal de Amor	VAls	"	05/22/1930
5618	De Flor en Flor	Tango	"	05/22/1930
5619	Por Seguidora y Por Fiel	Tango	"	05/22/1930
5633	Knockout de Amor	Tango	"	05/25/1930
5634	Canchero	Tango	"	05/25/1930
5740	Tarde Gris	Tango	"	06/17/1930
5741	Gacho Gris	Tango	"	06/17/1930
5742	Un Año Más	Tango	"	06/17/1930
5743	Tortazos	Milonga	"	06/17/1930
5792	La Pena del Payador	Vals	"	06/26/1930
5813	As de Cartón	Tango	"	06/28/1930
5814	Pordioseros	Tango	"	06/28/1930
5953	Incurable	Tango	"	08/21/1930
5954	Paquetín, Paquetón	Tango	"	08/21/1930
5955	En la Tranquera	Ranchera	"	08/21/1930
5956	Titiriteros	Tango	"	08/21/1930
5957	Colorao, Colorao	Tango	"	08/21/1930
5958	Chinita	Tango	"	08/21/1930
5960	Mañanita de Campo	Ranchera	"	08/26/1930
5961	No Llore, Viejita	Tango	"	08/28/1930

Master	Title	Genre	Accompaniment	Date
5962	Intimas	Tango	Guitars by Barbieri, Aguilar + Riverol	08/28/1930
5963	Padrino Pelao	Tango	"	08/28/1930
6052	El Quinielero	Tango	"	09/17/1930
6053	Fayuto	Tango	"	09/17/1930
6054	Mala Suerte	Vals	"	09/17/1930
6064	Clavel del Aire	Tango	"	09/19/1930
6065	La Violeta	Tango	"	09/19/1930
6066	La Pastelera	Ranchera	"	09/19/1930
6067	Caprichosa	Fado	"	09/19/1930
6094	Delirio Gaucho	Vals	"	09/25/1930
6095	Viva la Patria	Tango	"	09/25/1930
6126	La Mariposa	Tango	"	09/30/1930
6127	Viejo Rincón	Tango	"	09/30/1930
6128	Silbando	Tango	"	09/30/1930
6186	Murmullos	Tango	"	10/16/1930
6187	Farolito de Papel	Tango	"	10/16/1930
6188	Hágame el Favor	Tango	"	10/16/1930
6189	Yira, Yira	Tango	"	10/16/1930
6194	Recordando Mi Barrio	Vals	"	10/17/1930
6195	Anoche a las Dos	Tango	"	10/17/1930
6271	La Ultima Ronda	Vals	"	11/04/1930
6272	Araca, París	Tango	"	11/04/1930
6273	Llevame, Carretero	Tango	"	11/04/1930
6274	La Tropilla	Triunfo	"	11/04/1930
6275	Hay Una Virgen	Canción	"	11/04/1930
6449	Buey Manso	Tango	"	12/01/1930
6450	Pituca	Tango	"	12/01/1930
6451	Giuseppe, El Zapatero	Tango	"	12/01/1930
6452	Muchachos, Silencio	Tango	"	12/01/1930
6453	Como la Mosca	Tango	"	12/01/1930
6454	Las Flores de Tu Balcón	Pasodoble	"	12/01/1930
6484	La Mariposa	Tango	Francisco Canaro Orch	12/05/1930
6485	Rosas de Otoño	Vals	"	12/05/1930
6486	Senda Florida	Tango	"	12/05/1930
6487	Viejo Rincón	Tango	"	12/05/1930

Electrical Recordings for Odeón recorded by Gardel in Paris (1931)

Master	Title	Genre	Accompaniment	Date
Ki 4484	Querencia	Cifra	Guitars by Barbieri + Riverol	05/28/1931
Ki 4485	Anclao en París	Tango	"	05/28/1931
Ki 4486	Madre Hay Una Sola	Tango	"	05/28/1931

Master	Title	Genre	Accompaniment	Date
Ki 4487	Como Abrazado a un Rencor	Tango	Guitars by Barbieri + Riverol	05/28/1931
Ki 4488	Fondín de Pedro Mendoza	Tango	"	05/28/1931
Ki 4489	Gotas de Veneno	Tango	"	05/28/1931
Ki 4490	Hasta que Ardan los Candiles	Ranchera	"	05/28/1931
Ki 4491	Dejà	Vals	"	05/28/1931
Ki 4492	Folie	Canción	"	05/28/1931
Ki 4493	Riojana Mía	Vals	"	05/28/1931

Electrical Recordings for Odeón recorded by Gardel in Buenos Aires (1931)

Master	Title	Genre	Accompaniment	Date
6844	Confesión	Tango	Francisco Canaro Orchestra	09/03/1931
6845	Anclao en París	Tango	Guitars by Vivas, Barbieri + Riverol	09/04/1931
6846	Preparate P'al Domingo	Tango	"	09/04/1931
6847	Ofrenda Maleva	Tango	"	09/04/1931
6857	Esclavas Blancas	Tango	"	09/16/1931
6858	Como se Canta en Nápoles	Canción of Naples	"	09/16/1931
6859	Como Abrazado a un Rencor	Tango	"	09/16/1931
6871	Dejà	Vals	Gregor Kalikian Orchestra	09/21/1931
6872	Folie	Canción	"	09/21/1931
6873	Madame C'est Vous	Canción	"	09/21/1931
6874	Je Te Dirai	Canción	"	09/21/1931
6875	Cantar Eterno	Canción	Guitars by Vivas, Barbieri + Riverol	09/23/1931
6878	Tomo y Obligo	Tango	"	09/28/1931
6879	Flor del Valle	Tango	"	09/28/1931
6880	Trovas	Tango	"	09/28/1931
6915	Taconeando	Tango	Francisco Canaro Orch	10/26/1931
6916	Tomo y Obligo	Tango	"	10/26/1931
6917	Yo No Sé Que Me Han Hecho Tus Ojos	Vals	"	10/26/1931
6918	Falsas Promesas	Tango	Guitars by Vivas, Barbieri + Riverol	10/27/1931
6919	Madreselva	Tango	Francisco Canaro Orch	10/27/1931
6920	Quejas del Alma	Vals	Guitars by Vivas, Barbieri + Riverol	10/27/2031
6921	Quien Tuviera 18 Años	Tango	"	10/27/1931
6922	Ojos Maulas	Tango	"	10/27/1931

Electrical Recordings for Odeón recorded by Gardel in Barcelona (1932)

Master	Title	Genre	Accompaniment	Date
So 7789	Mentira	Tango	Piano and violin	07/22/1932
So 7790	Pan	Tango	"	07/22/1932
So 7791	Otario que Andás Penando	Tango	"	07/22/1932
So 7792	El Rosal	Canción	Piano and guitar	07/22/1932
So 7797	Por Favor Dejame	Tango	Piano and violin	07/23/1932
So 7798	Sueño Querido	Tango	"	07/23/1932
So 7799	Sueño de Juventud	Vals	Piano, violin, vibraphone	07/23/1932
So 7800	Noches de Montmartre	Tango	Piano and violin	07/23/1932
So 7801	Aquellas Cartas	Tango	"	07/23/1932
So 7802	Sorpresa	Tango	"	07/23/1932
So 7803	Mentiras	Tonada	Piano and guitar	07/23/1932
So 7804	Cara Rota	Tango	Piano and violin	07/23/1932

Electrical Recordings for Odeón recorded by Gardel in Buenos Aires (1933)

Master	Title	Genre	Voices	Accompaniment	Date
7318	Sueño Querido	Tango	Gardel	Guitars by Pettorossi, Barbieri, Riverol + Vivas	01/13/1933
7319	Mentiras	Tonada	"	"	01/13/1933
7320	Aquellas Cartas	Tango	"	"	01/13/1933
7321	Cara Rota	Tango	"	"	01/13/1933
7329	Milonga Sentimental	Milonga	"	"	01/23/1933
7330	Canción de Buenos Aires	Tango	"	"	01/23/1933
7331	Me Enamoré Una Vez	Ranchera	"	"	01/23/1933
7332	Secreto	Tango	"	"	01/23/1933
7333	Melodía de Arrabal	Tango	"	"	01/25/1933
7334	Rencor	Tango	"	"	01/25/1933
7342	Silencio	Tango	"	Guitars, trumpet and two female vocalists	02/14/1933
7344	Criollita de Mis Ensueños	Zamba	"	Guitars by Pettorossi, Barbieri, Riverol + Vivas	02/15/1933
7345	Ventarrón	Tango	"	"	02/15/1933
7350	Recuerdo Malevo	Tango	"	"	02/22/1933
7351	Acquaforte	Tango	"	"	02/22/1933
7352	Al Mundo le Falta un Tornillo	Tango	"	"	02/22/1933
7353	Me Da Pena Confesarlo	Tango	"	"	02/22/1933
7365	Parlez Moi D´amour	Canción	"	"	03/09/1933

Master	Title	Genre	Voices	Accompaniment	Date
7366	La Novia Ausente	Tango	"	Guitars by Pettorossi, Barbieri, Riverol + Vivas	03/09/1933
7382	Estudiante	Tango	"	Alberto Castellanos Orchestra	03/17/1933
7383	Cuando Tu No Estás	Canción	"	"	03/17/1933
7384	Por Tus Ojos Negros	Rumba	"	"	03/17/1933
7385	Silencio	Tango	"	Francisco Canaro Orchestra	03/27/1933
7426	Rumores	Canción	"	Guitars by Pettorossi, Barbieri, Riverol + Vivas	05/13/1933
7427	Silencio	Tango		" Guitars with female vocal chorus	05/13/1933
7428	Naipe Marcado	Tango	"	Guitars by Pettorossi, Barbieri, Riverol + Vivas	05/13/1933
7450	Araca la Cana	Tango	"	"	06/12/1933
7451	Milonga del 900	Milonga	"	"	06/12/1933
7452	Mis Flores Negras	Pasillo	"	"	06/12/1933
7468	Si se Salva el Pibe	Tango	"	"	06/17/1933
7469	Desdén	Tango	"	"	06/17/1933
7478	La Criolla	Canción	"	"	07/26/1933
7479	Para Quererte Nací	Cifra	"	"	07/26/1933
7480	Noches de Atenas	Vals	"	Alberto Castellanos Orchestra	07/31/1933
7508	La Uruguayita Lucía	Tango	"	Guitars by Pettorossi, Barbieri, Riverol + Vivas	08/25/1933
7509	Amante Corazón	Vals	"	"	08/25/1933
7510	Cobardía	Tango	"	"	08/25/1933
7511	Tenemos que Abrirnos	Tango	"	"	08/25/1933
7519	Mi Primer Gol	Tango	"	"	09/01/1933
7527	Cantar Eterno	Canción	Duet with himself	Guitars by Pettorossi, Barbieri, Riverol + Vivas	09/11/1933
7528	Rumores	Canción	"	"	09/11/1933
7532	Promesa	Vals	Gardel	"	09/13/1933
7533	Si Soy Así	Tango	"	"	09/13/1933
7538	Medallita de la Suerte (Mi Alhaja)	Tango	"	"	09/18/1933
7539	Al Pie de la Santa Cruz	Tango	"	"	09/18/1933
7540	Angustias	Tango	Duet with himself	"	09/18/1933
7541	Jujeña	Tonada	"	"	09/18/1933
7542	Mañanita de Sol	Canción	"	"	09/26/1933
7549	Ausencia	Vals	Gardel	"	10/13/1933
7550	Mi Manta Pampa	Zamba	"	"	10/01/1933
7551	Sanjuanina de Mi Amor	Zamba	Duet with himself	"	10/13/1933
7552	Una Rosa Para Mi Rosa	Canción	"	"	10/13/1933
7559	El que Atrasó el Reloj	Tango	Gardel	"	10/16/1933
7565	La Pastora	Canción	Duet with himself	"	10/19/1933

Master	Title	Genre	Voices	Accompaniment	Date
7566	La Madrugada	Canción	Duet with himself	Guitars by Pettorossi, Barbieri, Riverol + Vivas	10/19/1933
7580	Quimera	Tango	Gardel	"	11/02/1933
7581	Suena Guitarra Querida	Estilo	"	"	10/25/1933
7582	A Mí Madre (Con los Amigos)	Canción	"	"	10/25/1933
7584	Tu Diagnóstico	Vals	"	"	11/06/1933
7585	El Tirador Plateao	Estilo	"	"	11/06/1933
7586	Madame Ivonne	Tango	"	"	11/06/1933

Electrical Recordings for RCA Victor recorded by Gardel in New York (1934-1935)

Master	Title	Genre	Accompaniment	Date
BS 83591	Criollita Decí que Sí	Cifra	Guitars and piano	07/27/1934
BS 83592	Caminito Soleado	Zamba	"	07/27/1934
BS 83598	Cuesta Abajo	Tango	Terig Tucci Orchestra	07/30/1934
BS 83599	Mi Buenos Aires Querido	Tango	"	07/30/1934
BS 83700	Amores de Estudiante	Vals	"	07/30/1934
BS 83701	Golondrinas	Tango	"	07/30/1934
BS 83702	Soledad	Tango	"	07/30/1934
BS 83703	Rubias de Nueva York	Foxtrot	"	07/30/1934
BS 84129	Apure, Delantero Buey	Canción	"	08/24/1934
BS 84130	Amargura	Tango	"	08/24/1934
BVE 89224	Arrabal Amargo	Tango	"	03/19/1935
BVE 89225	Sus Ojos se Cerraron	Tango	"	03/19/1935
BVE 89226	Volver	Tango	"	03/19/1935
BVE 89227	Por una Cabeza	Tango	"	03/19/1935
BVE 89228	Lejana Tierra Mía	Canción	"	03/19/1935
BVE 89229	El Día que Me Quieras	Tango	"	03/19/1935
BVE 89230	Volvió una Noche	Tango	"	03/19/1935
BVE 89231	Sol Tropical (Amor Tropical)	Rumba	"	03/20/1935
BVE 89232	Los Ojos de Mi Moza	Jota	"	03/20/1935
BVE 89233	Cheating Muchachita	Tango	"	03/20/1935
BS 89235	Guitarra Mía	Canción Criolla	Guitars by Barbieri, Aguilar + Riverol	03/20/1935
BVE 89451	Spoken word recorded by Gardel	Saludo		03/25/1935

This discography was compiled with the invaluable collaboration of Manuel Llano, record collector and expert in the work of Carlos Gardel.

CHRONOLOGY
THE LIFE OF CARLOS GARDEL

1890: On December 11, the Municipal Hospital of St. Joseph de la Grave in Toulouse, France, registers the birth of Charles Romuald Gardes, child of an unknown father and Berthe Gardes, clothes presser, born in Toulouse and residing at Canon D'Arcole, 4. He was baptized the same day, and the ceremony recorded in the official ledger of the hospital chapel. The home where Berthe and her baby son Charles lived is still standing.

1893: Berthe Gardes arrives in Buenos Aires with her son Charles aboard the Portuguese steamship "Don Pedro". The Dirección General de Migraciones (National Migrations Office) notes on March 11: "... Number 121; Berthe Gardes, French, widow, 27 years old, clothes presser, Catholic, passport number 94. Number 122; Charles Gardes, French, 2 years old...".

Berthe moves into a boarding house at 162 Uruguay Street with her son. She begins to work in the pressing shop owned by Anais Beaux, another Frenchwoman, whose clientele includes a substantial number of theater artists.

1897: Gardel passes first grade in public school with a grade of very good. He stayed in public schools with excellent grades until he was 11.

1901: Enrolls at San Carlos primary school, part of the Arts and Trades school. He starts singing in children's choirs.

1910: Having completed his studies, he began to work as a messenger, watchmaker's apprentice, printer, illustrator, etc. Gardel stays away from home for extended periods twice, forcing his mother to file a missing persons report with the police. They were living then at 1914 Corrientes Street. He had been working hard at learning to play the guitar for some time. Worked as a tap dancer in larger theaters, as well as prop master and stagehand. Gardel attempts to sing "like Caruso" or "Titta Ruffo".

Starts to venture out around the Mercado de Abasto and the neighborhoods bordering it at the same time, singing *criollo* songs. His fame earns him a distinctive nickname: the "Morocho of Abasto". Changes his surname from Gardes to Gardel.

1911: His fame extends to other neighborhoods in town. Fans of the *criollo* song form bring Carlos Gardel together with José Razzano.

1912-13: Formation of the Gardel-Martino duo, Gardel-Martino-Razzano trio, and Gardel-Martino-Salinas-Razzano quartet. Tours of several cities in Buenos Aires province.

In early 1912, the first recordings of Carlos Gardel singing and accompanying himself on guitar are produced. The Gardel-Razzano duo sings at the famous restaurant-cabaret "Armenonville" at the end of 1913 and hired for a series of successful appearances.

1914: Performances in theaters in Buenos Aires and various provincial capitals in Argentina, either as between-acts entertainment during stage plays or as a featured attraction.

1915: The appearances at Buenos Aires theaters continue and the duo makes its debut in Montevideo to the sustained applause of a diverse audience. Tour of Brazil, where they encountered Enrico Caruso by chance, who discussed, praised, and offered Gardel advice about his voice.

Guitarist José Ricardo joins the duo. In a street violence incident in Buenos Aires, Gardel receives a gunshot wound that leaves a bullet embedded in his left lung. It will remain lodged there for the rest of his life.

1916: Appearances in Buenos Aires theaters augmented by guitarist José Ricardo. They now perform with the most important national and international artists. On August 20, the *Círculo de la Prensa* honors Ortega Munilla, Ortega y Gasset, and Eduardo Marquina with a performance by the Gardel-Razzano duo.

1917: Their public performances are increasingly high profile. The duo makes their first recordings for the Argentinean label Odeón. During May and June, Carlos Gardel stars in the filming of the silent movie *Flor de Durazno*. After that, at the Teatro Empire in Buenos Aires, he sings the first tango-song: *Mi Noche Triste*, lyrics written by Pascual Contursi to the music of the tango "Lita" composed by Samuel Castriota years before. The duo tours Chile, the interior of Argentina, and Uruguay.

1918: Performances in various cities in Uruguay and Argentina. The duo is involved in creating the Variety Artists Association. Tour with the Roberto Firpo Orchestra of various cities in Argentina.

1919: Montevideo, Rosario, Concordia, Córdoba, Tucumán, and Buenos Aires are among the cities that applaud Gardel-Razzano. The recording sessions continue. Gardel adds two tangos to his solo repertoire within the duo: *Flor de Fango* and *De Vuelta al Bulín*. Filming of the movie *La Loba* (now lost), in which Carlos Gardel was reputed to be the star.

1920: The duo stops performing for some time due to Razzano's throat operation. They return with extraordinary success and to great acclaim by the major newspapers of the era. They record numerous *criollo* songs; the tangos are increasingly present in the material Gardel sings. Guitarist José Ricardo continues accompanying them. Carlos Gardel meets the girl who would be his girlfriend for many years, Isabel del Valle. She was 14 at the time.

1921: Performances, tours... and the gym where Gardel works out regularly to lose weight. A second guitarist, Guillermo Desiderio Barbieri, joins the group. He will accompany Gardel for more years than any other musician during his entire career.

1922: Sings at a special evening performance for Argentinean intellectuals and Jacinto Benavente from Spain. Appearances in theaters and recordings feature a greater number of tangos performed by Gardel as a soloist.

1923: Performance at theaters in Argentinean cities and Montevideo. The duo travels to Spain with the Rivera-De Rosas theater company. They appear at the Teatro Apolo in Madrid.

1924: They continue in Madrid with the Rivera-De Rosas company through mid-January. The duo travels to Toulouse to visit Gardel's relatives and then immediately move on to Paris. They return to Buenos Aires and record for Odeón. The preeminence of Gardel as a soloist and tango singer is observed and noted. First performances on radio.

1925: Landmark year in his career. A decrease in José Razzano's presence as a singer, due to weakening of his vocal cords, is apparent in both theater appearances and recordings. Gardel becomes the owner of the racehorse "Lunático" and a close friend of jockey Irineo Leguisamo and trainer Francisco Maschio. The duo sings for the Prince of Wales, representative of the British Empire, when he visits Argentina.

In October Gardel and Razzano go their separate ways as artists and performers. Nonetheless, Gardel signs a general power of attorney for José Razzano to administer his affairs and the profits from his artistic career. Razzano will continue sharing a 50% split with his old duo partner.

Gardel travels to Spain accompanied by guitarist José Ricardo. He performs in Barcelona and Madrid with the Rivera-De Rosas company again. He records for the Odeón label in Spain.

1926: Continues in Madrid, filling the Teatro Romea to capacity for a month despite predictions of low turn-out due to the *cuesta de enero* (lack of money after holiday spending). Records more disks in Barcelona.

Returns to Buenos Aires in March where he continues recording a repertoire now dominated by tangos. Gardel starts up live appearances in Buenos Aires theaters again that make an extraordinary impact on the general public and press. In November, he makes his first electrical recordings for the Odeón label, accompanied by Ricardo and Barbieri on guitar.

1927: The number of recordings using the electrical system multiply rapidly, with tangos forming an overwhelming majority of the repertoire.

The perfectionist Gardel does multiple takes of some songs until satisfied with the recorded results. Performs accompanied by his guitarists in halls in Montevideo, Buenos Aires and other Argentinean cities. In October, he travels to Spain with his two guitarists for the third time to perform onstage in Barcelona and Madrid.

1928: Recording sessions and radio appearances are added on top of the concert performances in Barcelona, Bilbao, San Sebastián, Santander and other cities.

Returns to Buenos Aires with contract in hand to perform in Paris. Gardel declares to the daily newspaper Crítica: "...I did a seven-month tour but I could have stayed out on the road for seven years (...) I came here because I felt a great need to return to see my own people, our own Buenos Aires, that we miss so much when we're away. And finally to record disks, study and prepare the latest new material before presenting myself to the Paris audience".

They continue their performances in halls in Buenos Aires and Montevideo. Starting in July, he adds a third guitarist for live appearances, radio performances and recordings. His name is José María Aguilar. In September, he embarks from Buenos Aires, en route to Paris with his three guitarists. Thanks to the powerful

SINGS AT FLORIDA

Carlos Gardel, celebrated Argentine singer who is now engaged at "The Florida" in Paris where he sings every evening. His engagement has been marked by tremendous success.

impresario Paul Santolini, Gardel makes his debut at the Fémina Theater and then appears at the Florida dance cabaret for four months. The decor of the latter venue was specially designed to highlight the singer. Starts recording a series of disks in Paris for the Odeón label.

1929: Sings at the Paris Opera House on an impressive bill of artists including Mistinguett, Chevalier, Lucien Boyer, Raimú, Lis Coty, and the tango orchestra of Fresedo. Performances in Cannes and once again in Paris. Appearances in Barcelona and Madrid. Cuts his ties with José Ricardo. Return to Buenos Aires, exultant over his success and eager to continue working. Sings in halls and radio stations in Buenos Aires and Montevideo. Records extensively with his two guitarists. Now living at 735 Jean Jaurés Street in Buenos Aires, famous today as the "Carlos Gardel House".

1930: Touring cities in Argentina. Appearances in halls in Buenos Aires and on radio with a new guitarist on board: Angel Domingo Riverol. Numerous recordings continuing to give a featured role to the many tangos in his repertoire.

Filming of *Encuadre de Canciones*, the first Argentinean sound movie with Carlos Gardel in the starring role. He sings 15 songs that were already famous, and 11 of them are preserved today. He is accompanied by his three guitarists and/or the Francisco Canaro Orchestra. In December, he travels again to Paris to appear at the Empire Theater.

1931: Sings in Nice, Cannes, and Monte Carlo with his three guitarists until late March, when Aguilar abandons the tour. Gardel subsequently begins his period of peak movie activity by filming *Luces de Buenos Aires* in Joinville, Paris, while continuing his performances at the Palace Theater and recording sessions.

He returns to Buenos Aires in July after his commitments are completed. Appearances in theaters, on radio, and recordings. A new guitarist is added: Domingo Julio Vivas. Disagreements come to the fore with José Razzano, who had badly mismanaged the last years of Gardel's career. Gardel begins to entrust his business affairs to Armando Defino.

1932: Back in Europe without his musicians and full of great expectations to film for Paramount Pictures due to the box-office success of *Luces de Buenos Aires*. Not the best timing, though, as the company is suffering a financial crisis and suspends all its filming activity in Europe. Gardel continues his trip for vacations and in search of new horizons for his art in London, Rome, Naples, Nice, and Paris again. There he begins his fruitful collaboration with Battistella and Alfredo Le Pera, who will remain a permanent fixture in the singer's future artistic career. Filming of *Espérame, La Casa es Seria* (short) and *Melodía de Arrabal,* with lyrics by Le Pera and music by Gardel. Returns to Buenos Aires in December.

1933: His last stay in Buenos Aires. Numerous recording sessions accompanied by the guitars of Barbieri, Riverol, Vivas and new addition Horacio Pettorossi. He is no less active with performances in various cities in Argentina and Uruguay, both in theaters and on radio broadcasts.

Revokes whatever power José Razzano may retain over his affairs. Appoints Armando Defino his manager. Before leaving for Europe again, he drafts his handwritten will.

With Le Pera and Defino in Paris, he outlines a potential new project to shoot at the film studios Paramount owns in New York. He arrives there on December 27. Gardel rehearses with a 17-piece orchestra, conducted by Hugo Mariani and including violinist/arranger Terig Tucci among the musicians, for his debut on the powerful NBC radio network.

1934: Continues with the NBC broadcasts. Films "Cuesta Abajo" and "Tango on Broadway". Begins to record the songs from his movies for the RCA Victor label, with lyrics by Alfredo Le Pera and music composed primarily by Gardel himself.

Sings for audiences in Argentina, Uruguay, Canada, Brazil and other countries through the connection established by NBC with other radio broadcasters. Now he is the most important tango singer for both national and foreign audiences. His films make his fame and popularity as a performer take off in the entire Spanish-speaking world. He stars in segments of the film "The Big Broadcast of 1935" *(Cazadores de Estrellas)*. Prepares the screenplays, lyrics and music of his future films with Le Pera.

1935: Filming of *El Día que Me Quieras*. He summons the guitarists Barbieri, Riverol and Aguilar so they can accompany him on upcoming tours. Filming of "Tango Bar". Recordings with the Terig Tucci orchestra. Begins what would be his final tour, with appearances in Puerto Rico, the Lesser Antilles, and several cities in Venezuela and Colombia. The performances are greeted with an unprecedented wave of popular and press acclaim. Gardel is definitively "The King of Tango".

At 3.10 pm on June 24, in Medellin, Colombia, a tragic collision between two airplanes ends his life along with 17 other people. Among the bodies are two of Gardel's guitarists, Guillermo Desiderio Barbieri and Angel Domingo Riverol, and the screenwriter of his films and author of the lyrics to his last songs, Alfredo Le Pera.

The displays of grief and sorrow are extraordinary in different locations around the world. On February 5, 1936, his remains are moved to Buenos Aires where an impressive crowd in mourning pays tribute to the singer and accompanies the burial in the La Chacarita cemetery. The truth and legend of Carlos Gardel is now set in motion, surpassing all predictions in a world of followers and collectors encompassing even the most unexpected corners of the world.

CARLOS GARDEL FAMILY TREE

RAMA TOULOUSIANA

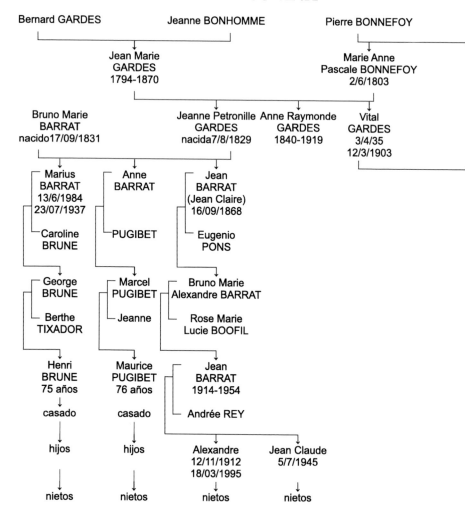

Bernard GARDES   Jeanne BONHOMME   Pierre BONNEFOY

Jean Marie
GARDES
1794-1870

Marie Anne
Pascale BONNEFOY
2/6/1803

Bruno Marie
BARRAT
nacido17/09/1831

Jeanne Petronille
GARDES
nacida7/8/1829

Anne Raymonde
GARDES
1840-1919

Vital
GARDES
3/4/35
12/3/1903

Marius
BARRAT
13/6/1984
23/07/1937

Anne
BARRAT

Jean
BARRAT
(Jean Claire)
16/09/1868

Caroline
BRUNE

PUGIBET

Eugenio
PONS

George
BRUNE

Marcel
PUGIBET

Bruno Marie
Alexandre BARRAT

Berthe
TIXADOR

Jeanne

Rose Marie
Lucie BOOFIL

Henri
BRUNE
75 años
↓
casado
↓
hijos
↓
nietos

Maurice
PUGIBET
76 años
↓
casado
↓
hijos
↓
nietos

Jean
BARRAT
1914-1954

Andrée REY

Alexandre
12/11/1912
18/03/1995
↓
nietos

Jean Claude
5/7/1945
↓
nietos

RAMA ALBIGEOISE

Antoinette CAZENEUVE

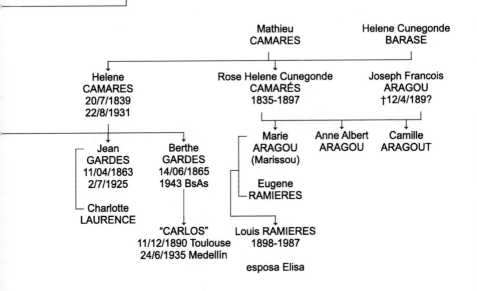

LUNFARDO GLOSSARY

A la sombra: In jail.

Acamalar: To keep/support a woman

Afanar: Rob, steal

Amurar: Leave, abandon

Apoliyar: Sleep

Atorrar: Sleep

Bacán/a: Individual with lavish lifestyle

Balconear: To observe, look at

Batir: To say, reveal, disclose

Batuque: Noisy party

Berretín: Whim, desire

Biscuit: Flirtatious woman

Botón: Cop

Bulín: Room, apartment of a single man

Cabrero: Angry, upset

Cafishio: Pimp

Camba: Individual with modest lifestyle (see bacán)

Camorra: Fight, argument

Campanear: Spy on

Catre/Catrera: Bed

Cotorro: Room, especially for a single man

Chamuyo: Confidential conversation

Chivar: Betray

Chorro: Robber

Chufa: Horchata de chufa

Dique: Arrogance, pretentiousness

Diquero: arrogant, pretentious

Embretar: Get someone in trouble

Encanar: Put in jail

Encurdelarse: Get drunk

Engrupir: Deceive

Espiantar: Take someone away from a place

Estufar: Bore, annoy

Farra: Fun, good times, party hearty

Fayar: Fail to keep your word

Fuelle: Lung, bandoneón

Fulero: Bad, evil

Funghi: Hat

Garufa: Party person

Gavión: Ladies man, seducer

Gil: Stupid

Gotan: is a variant spelling of tango, created for rhyme and

poetic reasons
Grela: Woman
Grupo: Trick, lie
Guapo: Brave guy
Junar: To observe, look at
Macana: Mistake, bad idea
Malevo: Outlaw
Malevaje: Outlaws
Mango: Unit of currency.
Manyar: Understand, perceive
Marchanta: Waste
Mate: Head
Matungo: Horse
Maula: Coward, deceitful
Metejón: Fall in love
    obsessively
Mina: Woman
Mistongo/a: Humble, poor,
    miserable
Morfar: Eat
Morlaco: Argentinian peso
Otario: Naive, stupid, sucker
Pago: Place where you come
    from
Paica: Young woman
    intimately involved in
    tango world
Paquete: Unattractive woman
Parlar: Talk
Patinar: Waste, use up
Pebeta: Young woman
Percanta: Woman
Piantar: See Espiantar
Pibe: Young boy, teenage boy,
    kid

Pierna: Close friend, like a
    brother
Pingo: Horse
Piña: Blow, punch
Piolín: Kite string
Pique: Day job
Planchar: Young girl stood
    up for a dance
Prepo: Arrogance
Pucho: Cigarette butt
Rana: Astute, shrewd person,
    swindler, con man
Rante: Wanderer, streetwise
    person
Rechiflarse: Become
    obsessed, enraged
Remanyar: Embrace an idea
Tamango: Shoe or boot
Tano: Italian
Taura: Bold, brave
Tovén: Money
Tungo: Horse
Turro: Bad person
Vedera / Vereda: Sidewalk
Vento: Money (see tovén)
Ventolina: Money
Vuaturé: Light automobile
Yirar: Roam
Yobaca: Horse
Zabeca: Head

TRANSLATOR NOTES ABOUT LYRICS:

** All translations of lyrics obviously are approximate, aiming to give an idea of what the song is about and hopefully with some poetic flavor.

AUTHOR / TRANSLATOR NOTES:

Río de la Plata/ rioplatense

The Río de la Plata forms part of the border between Argentina and Uruguay. Rioplatense refers to the common culture that developed along both coasts, centered around the capital cities of Buenos Aires and Montevideo, and spread to other cities like Rosario, Bahía Blanca, etc., which also became important centers for tango.

Suburbs/ suburban

Suburbs and suburban are used here in the South American / European sense. They are not the affluent enclaves of the United States / North America for living at a safe distance from the big city. These suburbs are the communities that formed on the outskirts around the wealthy central nucleus of South American cities. They are poor, more marginal neighborhoods populated by immigrants from overseas or the countryside.

Lunfardo

Argentinean slang created and developed in Buenos Aires.

Orilla / Orillero / Arrabal

Orilla is used here to mean the outskirts of a city center. Orillero refers to someone from the margins, whether for the location where they live or in terms of social status. Arrabal is a suburban community, more like a neighborhood/ barrio.

Criollo

Individual born in Latin America with at least one parent of European descent. That may include children of two Spanish parents, one intermixed with natives of other European countries.

Orchestra / Sexteto Típico

Orchestra is used here to indicate any backing group of tango musicians, not necessarily a large ensemble. The traditional core is piano, violin, contrabass and bandoneon but the exact instrumentation depends on the individual preference of the bandleader. The Sexteto Típico was the classic line-up during the years of Gardel's career but Gardel preferred the guitar for accompaniment over orchestral groups.

Criollo song tradition

Original material from rural Argentina with some element of European song styles incorporated. It is based on fixed forms.

Folk/ Folklórico

Original songs from rural Argentina but exclusively from indigenous styles, also based on fixed forms. From the word folklórico, a descriptive classification frequently used in Spanish-language music writing that doesn't conform exactly to the North American concepts of folk music and/or folklore.

Payador

Folk singers who drew on rural Argentinean life and sources for material but improvised their lyrics in the moment during their performances. The improvisation separates the payadores from the other types of music described above.

Canción / song

Any composition not clearly accompanied by tango or folk music.

Tango-song

A tango with a poem or lyric added for singing.

National song/ singer

An artist who draws on the full range of the Argentinean national songbook, rural and urban, taking material from any of the song styles described above.

THIRD PART

BIBLIOGRAPHY

VARIOUS AUTHORS. *Tango, magia y realidad.* Corregidor,
Buenos Aires, 1998.

VARIOUS AUTHORS. *La Historia del Tango.* Serie de 19 vols,
Corregidor, Buenos Aires, 1976.

VARIOUS AUTHORS. *Tango 1880, Un siglo de historia.*
Corregidor, Buenos Aires, 1980.

ALEN LASCANO, Luis. *La Argentina ilusionada.* La Bastilla,
Buenos Aires, 1977.

ANDRADE, Juan Carlos y SAN MARTÍN, Horacio. *Del debute
chamuyar canero.* Peña Lillo. Buenos Aires, 1967.

ASSUNÇAO, Fernando. *El tango y sus circunstancias.* El Ateneo,
Buenos Aires, 1984.

AYESTARÁN, Lauro. *El Folklore musical uruguayo.* Arca,
Montevideo, 1967.

AZZI, María Susana. *Antropología del tango; los protagonistas.*
Olavarría, Buenos Aires, 1991.

BARCIA, José. *Discepolín.* Centro Editor de América Latina,
Buenos Aires, 1971.

BARCIA, José, FULLE Enriqueta y NIACOGGI José Luis.
Primer diccionario Gardeliano. Corregidor, Bs. Aires, 1991.

BARREIRO, Javier. *El tango hasta Gardel.* Diputación Provincial
de Zaragoza, Zaragoza, 1986.

BATES, Luis Héctor. *La historia del tango (primera parte).* Fabril
Editora, Buenos Aires, 1936.

BAUDELAIRE, Charles. *Escritos íntimos.* Universidad de
Murcia, Murcia, 1994.

BORGES, Jorge Luis. *Obras completas.* Emecé, Buenos Aires,
1989.

CADÍCAMO, Enrique. *Poemas del bajo fondo (Viento que lleva y
trae).* Peña Lillo, Buenos Aires, 1964.

CADÍCAMO, Enrique. *Cancionero.* Torres Agüero Editor,
Buenos Aires, 1977.

CADÍCAMO, Enrique. *Gardel en París: su debut.* Corregidor,
Buenos Aires, 1984.

CANARO, Francisco. *Mis bodas de oro con el tango*. Buenos Aires, 1957.

CARELLA, Tulio. *El tango, mito y esencia*. Doble P, Buenos Aires, 1956.

CARRETERO, Andrés V. *Tango, testigo social*. JA Roca, Buenos Aires, 1996.

CARRIEGO, Evaristo. *Misas herejes*. Tor, Buenos Aires, 1946.

CHINARRO, Andrés. *El tango y su rebeldía*. Continental Service, Buenos Aires, 1965.

COLLIER, Simón. *Carlos Gardel, su vida, su música, su época*. Sudamericana, Buenos Aires, 1992.

CONTURSI, Pascual y CONTURSI, José María. *Cancionero*. Torres Agüero Editor, Buenos Aires, 1977.

CORSINI, Ignacio (H). *Ignacio Corsini, mi padre*. Todo es historia, Buenos Aires, 1979.

CORTÁZAR, Julio. *La vuelta al mundo en ochenta días*. Siglo XXI de España editores, Madrid, 1984.

DEFINO, Armando. *Carlos Gardel (la verdad de una vida)*. Fabril Editora, Buenos Aires, 1968.

DE CARO, Julio. *El tango en mis recuerdos*. Centurión, Buenos Aires, 1964.

DEL PRIORE, Óscar and others. *2x4=Tango*. Grupo Editor de Buenos Aires, 1980.

DINZEL, Rodolfo. *El tango, una danza*. Corregidor, 1994.

DISCÉPOLO, Enrique Santos. *Cancionero*. Torres Agüero Editor, Buenos Aires, 1977.

EICHELBAUM, Edmundo. *El discurso gardeliano. La historia del tango*. Corregidor, Buenos Aires, 1977.

ERNIÉ, Héctor. *Carlos Gardel en su centenario*. Tango, Buenos Aires, 1990.

ETCHEBARNE, Miguel D. *La influencia del arrabal en la poesía argentina culta*. Kraft, Buenos Aires, 1955.

ESTEBAN, Juan Carlos. *Carlos Gardel, encuadre histórico*. Corregidor, Buenos Aires, 2001.

EXPÓSITO, Homero. *Cancionero*. Torres Agüero Editor, Buenos Aires, 1978.

FERRER, Horacio. *El tango, su historia y evolución.* Peña Lillo, Buenos Aires, 1960.

FLORES, Celedonio. *Chapaleando barrio.* El Maguntino, Buenos Aires, 1951.

FLORES Celedonio. *Cancionero.* Torres Agüero Editor, Buenos Aires, 1977.

FLORES, Rafael. *Carlos Gardel, tango inacabable.* Ediciones G y C, Madrid, 1997.

FLORES, Rafael. *El tango, desde el umbral hacia dentro.* Catriel, Madrid, 1997.

FLORES, Rafael. *Gardel y el tango.* Repertorio de recuerdos. Ediciones de la Tierra, Madrid, 2001.

FORD, Aníbal. *Homero Manzi.* Centro Editor de América Latina, Buenos Aires, 1971.

FRATANTONI, César. *Mundo Gardeliano Blog.*

GALASSO, Norberto. *Discépolo y su época.* Jorge Álvarez, Buenos Aires, 1967.

GALASSO, Norberto. *Escritos Inéditos de Enrique Santos Discépolo.* Editorial del Pensamiento Nacional, Bs. As., 1981.

GÁLVEZ, Manuel. *Historia del arrabal.* Hachette, Bs .As., 1956.

GARCÍA JIMÉNEZ, Francisco. *Vida de Carlos Gardel contada por José Razzano.* Buenos Aires, 1951.

GARCÍA JIMÉNEZ, Francisco. *El tango: Historia de medio siglo 1880-1930.* Eudeba, Buenos Aires, 1965.

GARCÍA JIMÉNEZ, Francisco. *Cancionero.* Torres Agüero Editor, Buenos Aires, 1978.

GOBELLO, José. Lunfardía. *Acotaciones al lenguaje porteño.* Argos, Buenos Aires, 1953.

GOBELLO, José. *Diccionario Lunfardo.* Peña Lillo, Buenos Aires, 1977.

GOBELLO, José. *Crónica general del tango.* Fraterna, Buenos Aires, 1980.

GOBELLO, José. *Tres estudios gardelianos.* Academia Porteña de Lunfardo, Buenos Aires, 1991.

GOLDAR, Ernesto. *La mala vida.* Centro Editor de América Latina, Buenos Aires, 1971.

GÓMEZ DE LA SERNA, Ramón. *Interpretación del tango.*
Albino y Asociados, Buenos Aires, 1979.

GONZÁLEZ CASTILLO, José y CASTILLO Cátulo.
Cancionero. Torres Agüero Editor, Buenos Aires, 1977.

DEL GRECO, Orlando. *Carlos Gardel, los autores de sus
canciones.* Akián, Buenos Aires, 1990.

GUTIÉRREZ MIGLIO, Roberto. *El tango y sus intérpretes.*
Corregidor, Buenos Aires, 1994.

HERNÁNDEZ, Anastasio. *Vida y obra de Carlos Gardel.*
Ediciones de autor. Córdoba, Argentina, 1996.

HUET, Héctor. *Carlos Gardel, el detalle que faltaba.* Corregidor,
Buenos Aires, 1995.

IELPI, Rafael y ZINNI, Héctor. *Prostitución y rufianismo.*
Ediciones de la Bandera, Buenos Aires, 1986.

DE LARA, Tomás y RONCETTI DE PANTI, Inés. *El tema del
tango en la literatura argentina.* Ediciones Culturales
Argentinas, Buenos Aires, 1961.

LASTRA F. Amadeo. *Recuerdos del 900.* Huemul, Bs. As., 1961.

LEFCOVICH S. Nicolás. *Estudio de la discografía de Carlos
Gardel.* Buenos Aires, 1988.

LEONARDO, Sergio. *La verdad y leyenda del tango en París.* La
Prensa, Buenos Aires, 15 de marzo de 1953.

LE PERA, Alfredo. *Cancionero.* Torres Agüero Editor, Buenos
Aires, 1980.

LE PERA, José. *Carlos Gardel, sus amigos, su última gira.*
Corregidor, Buenos Aires, 1991.

MANZI, Homero. *Cancionero.* Torres Agüero Editor, Buenos
Aires, 1977.

MARAMBIO CATÁN, Carlos. *60 años de tango (el tango que yo
viví).* Freeland, Buenos Aires, 1973.

MARECHAL, Leopoldo. *Historia de la calle Corrientes.*
Municipalidad de Buenos Aires, 1937.

MATAMORO, Blas. *La ciudad del tango (tango histórico y
sociedad).* Galerna, Buenos Aires, 1982.

MORENA, Miguel Angel. *Historia Artística de Carlos Gardel.*
Freeland, Buenos Aires, 1976.

NATALE, Oscar. *Buenos Aires, negros y tango*. Peña Lillo, Buenos Aires, 1984.

NOGUÉS, Germinal. *Buenos Aires, ciudad secreta*. Ruy Díaz-Sudamericana, Buenos Aires, 1993.

ONEGA, Gladys. *La inmigración en la literatura argentina 1880-1910*. Galerna, Buenos Aires, 1969.

ORTIZ, Fernando. *Glosario de afronegrismos*. Editorial de ciencias sociales, La Habana, 1990.

OSTUNI, Ricardo. *Repatriación de Gardel*. Club de Tango. Buenos Aires, 1995.

PÁEZ, Jorge. *El conventillo*. Centro Editor de América Latina. Buenos Aires, 1976.

PAYET, Luciano y GOBELLO, José. *Breve Diccionario de Lunfardo*. Peña Lillo, Buenos Aires, 1959.

PELUSO, Hamlet y VISCONTI, Eduardo. *Carlos Gardel y la prensa mundial*. Corregidor, Buenos Aires, 1990.

PELLETTIERI, Osando. *Radiografía de Carlos Gardel*. Ediciones Abril SA, Buenos Aires, 1985.

PORTALET, Ernesto. *El tango en España*. Corregidor, Buenos Aires, 1996.

PUGA, Boris. *Discografía de Carlos Gardel*. Club de la Guardia Nueva, Montevideo, 1970.

PUJOL, Sergio. *Jazz al sur*. Emecé, Buenos Aires, 1992.

QUINTANA, Federico. *En torno a lo argentino*. Coni, Buenos Aires, 1941.

RIMBAUD, Arthur. *Cartas Abisinias*.

RIVERO, Edmundo. *Las voces. Gardel y el canto*. Ediciones de autor, Buenos Aires, 1985.

ROMANO, Eduardo. *Sobre poesía popular Argentina*. Centro Editor de América Latina, Buenos Aires, 1983.

ROMANO, Eduardo. *Las letras del tango*. Fundación Ross, Buenos Aires, 1989.

ROMERO, Manuel. *Cancionero*. Torres Agüero Editor, Buenos Aires, 1978.

ROSSI, Vicente. *Cosas de negros*. Hachette, Buenos Aires, 1958.

ROSSI, Vicente. *Teatro nacional rioplatense*. Contribución a su análisis e historia. Hachette, Buenos Aires, 1969.

ROSSLER, Osvaldo. *Buenos Aires dos por cuatro*. Losada, Buenos Aires, 1967.

SÁBATO, Ernesto. T*ango, discusión y clave*. Losada, Buenos Aires, 1963.

SALAS, Horacio. *El tango*. Planeta, Buenos Aires, 1986.

SIERRA, Luis Adolfo. *Historia de la orquesta típica (Evolución testimonial del tango)*. Peña Lillo, Buenos Aires, 1966.

SIERRA, Luis Adolfo y FERRER Horacio. *Discepolín*. Tiempo, Buenos Aires, 1965.

SILVA, CABRERA Erasmo (Avlis). *Carlos Gardel el gran desconocido*. Ciudadela, Montevideo, 1967.

SOLER CAÑAS, Luis. *Negros, gauchos y compadres en el cancionero de la Federación 1830-1848*. Theoría, Bs .As., 1958.

SPERATTI, Alberto. *Con Piazzolla*. Galerna, Buenos Aires, 1969.

TALLÓN, José Sebastián. *El tango en sus etapas de música prohibida*. Amigos del libro argentino. Buenos Aires, 1964.

THOMAS, Vincent. *El Gardel que yo conocí*. Mundo Gardeliano Editions. 2015.

TUCCI, Terig. *Gardel en Nueva York*. Web Press, New York, 1969.

TURON, Ana. Museo del Libro *Gardel y su Tiempo*

UMANA, Mauricio y Manuela. *La Verdad sobre la muerte de Carlos Gardel*. Librería Jurídica Diké S.A.S. 2019.

VEGA, Carlos. *Danzas y canciones argentinas. Teorías e investigaciones*. Establecimiento Gráfico de E. Ferrero, Buenos Aires 1936.

VILLARIÑO, Idea. *Tango*. Arca, Montevideo, 1967.

VILLARIÑO, Idea. *Tangos, antología*. Centro Editor de América Latina, Buenos Aires, 1981.

YÉPEZ-POTTIER, Arturo. *La lágrima en la garganta*. Producciones El Copihue. 2017.

ZATTI, Rodolfo Omar. *Gardel y el Turf*. Corregidor, Buenos Aires, 1990.

ZINELLI, Carlos. *Carlos Gardel. El resplandor y la sombra*. Corregidor, Buenos Aires, 1987.

BOOKS BY THE AUTHOR ABOUT THE WORLD OF TANGO

"Carlos Gardel, Tango Inacabable"; Carlos Gardel, Tango Senza Fine; Carlos Gardel, Unendlicher Tango; Carlos Gardel, Tango à l'Infini*

*"El Tango desde el Umbral hacia Adentro"; *Il Tango e i suoi Labirinti*

*"Carlos Gardel y el Tango, Repertorio de Recuerdos"

*"Amor en el Tango, Gricel- José María Contursi"

*"Carlos Gardel, la Voz del Tango"; *Carlos Gardel, The Voice the of the Tango*

*"Osvaldo Berlingieri, Yo Toco el Piano"; "O. Berlingieri, Tôi cho'i dân du`o`ng câm"

*"Dioniso en la Fiesta del Tango"; "Dioniso nell´Abbraccio del Tango"

Book Introductions:

"Ramón Gómez de la Serna, Interpretación del Tango"
"El Chango Carmen"
"El Tango con Darío"
"Jorge Luis Borges y el Tango"
"Poetas del Tango y el Sentir Argentino"

Literary Work:

• Novel: "Otumba"

• Poetry: "De Aquello que Pasa y Queda"; "La Caracola en el Oído"; "El Oro de la Vida"; "Con el Hueco de la Mano hacia Arriba"

• Short Stories: "El Fin del Camino"; "En una Caja Oscura"; "Conversaciones con el Búho"; "Cuentos de Sombra Errante"; "De Padre, Madre y Otros Cuentos"

• Essays: "Pasión y Caída de los Gremios en Lucha"; "Semblanzas, Prólogos y Vivencias".

Further information:

www.rafaelfloresmontenegro.com
rafaelflores533@hotmail.com

ACKNOWLEDGEMENTS

The author would like to express his gratitude to his brotherly friend, record collector and expert in the work of Carlos Gardel, **Manuel Llano**, for the invaluable collaboration in the discography compilation; to the night owl **Donald Snowden**, excellent translator and jazz lover, for his dedication and efforts beyond the sun; and to **Santiago García**, philologist and rock'n roller, for his enthusiasm and soulful contribution to conveying the poetic significance of this work.

I would also want to thank **Silvia García Rey**, whose efforts and special care was vital in making this book a reality.

MUNDO GARDELIANO is the effort by a small group of people in Los Angeles, CA, to support writers, scholars, and anyone who is interested in information concerning the life and career of Carlos Gardel. We have visited collections and libraries around the world to accumulate what is probably the most comprehensive digital library there is regarding the great artist. We are present on the internet with our MUNDO GARDELIANO blog and on Facebook through the popular Pagina Gardeliana profile. Please feel free to contact us if you need assistance regarding the great artist.

Made in the USA
Middletown, DE
06 February 2020